MISSION WISE

SCRIPTURE, SCIENCE, AND SERVING
THE WORLD'S MOST VULNERABLE

MISSION WISE

JASON JOHNSON AND NICOLE WILKE
LAURA NZIRIMU, EDITOR

credo
house publishers

Published in the United States by Credo House Publishers,
a division of Credo Communications, LLC, Grand Rapids, Michigan

credohousepublishers.com

For more information, please visit missionwisebook.com.

ISBN: 978-1-62586-210-5

Cover and interior design by Frank Gutbrod

Cover illustrations by Freepik.com

Editing by Elizabeth Banks

Printed in the United States of America

First edition

CONTENTS

START HERE

Who Should Read This Book?

This book is uniquely written for anyone involved in their church's global engagement decision-making process. Whether you're on staff as a missions pastor, a volunteer on a missions committee, or a passionate advocate that helps bring global awareness and opportunities to your church leadership, this book is for you.

Why Should I Read This Book?

As a leader involved with much of the outreach and missions ministries of your church, you have many people, ideas, and priorities vying for your time. Your attention is a valuable commodity! So why should you spend a precious hour or two diving into the content of this resource?

Our goal with this information isn't to *spend* your time but to *save* it. There is an overwhelming number of nonprofit organizations in the world today, and chances are, many of them are knocking on your door. They want time, money, engagement, volunteers . . . in a word, they want your partnership. And partnership can be a wonderful thing!

There's also an overwhelming amount of information about how to best care for orphans and vulnerable children. Yet a lot of that information is hidden away in heady research papers or buried in the technical jargon of psychology textbooks. Not only that, but it's likely that if you have been involved in global missions for some length of time, the landscape of what we know about engaging globally has shifted over time, with more in-depth research and best-practice principles available now than ever before.

So how do you—a missions pastor, outreach minister, or someone in a leadership position responsible for making decisions about how your church will engage globally—sift through all the organizations and information to find a partnership that allows your congregation to serve vulnerable children, families, and communities most effectively? How do you effectively evaluate, encourage, and improve the partnerships you already have? You want to engage with your global (and local) partners with clarity, effectiveness, and maximum impact. You likely assess the theology of any new partners—but how do you assess their philosophy and methodology?

We want to help you take the guesswork out of that process. This book will walk through the basics of what we call "best practice"—research-based facts on the best way to engage globally, and more specifically, care for vulnerable children. You'll find practical ways to evaluate and improve your current partnerships, while at the same time developing a simple framework to honestly assess new partnerships and find the best fit.

So to answer the question of why you should read this book—you shouldn't! Instead, you should *use* this book. More than being read, it's designed to be used as a resource that you can refer to again and again throughout your journey. We pray this book is more than words on a page, but that it's a tool that will sit on your desk rather than on a shelf and be referred back to frequently as you serve in your role. While it won't answer every question, it will hopefully spark new ones as you process what best practice looks like in your own sphere of influence.

We see your heart to serve and to serve well. We believe you'll walk away with increased confidence in how God is calling your church to answer His call, and increased clarity on how to serve the vulnerable in a way that promotes their flourishing for His glory.

The time you invest in engaging with resources like this one reveals the worth you see in orphans and vulnerable children around the world. Thank you!

On Whiplash and Grace

Just like many aspects of life as a follower of Jesus, global orphan care is best done in community. And this resource is best utilized in a team context! While you may be reading it alone at first, processing through the implications of this information and their potential impact must be done with others on your missions and church team.

However, this is often where we encounter a dilemma. It's the adult version of a "youth camp high." When we attend a conference, it's easy to come home riding the wave of emotion and new information. *Everything looks different! Nothing should stay the same!* Often, most of these changes would be good—in moderation and in the right time. But to enter our next staff meeting with an onslaught of new ideas to implement can actually be detrimental to the success of the very changes we want to make.

The same tendency can occur when we encounter a resource like this one. *This information makes so much sense! Why didn't we do it this way before? Everything must change—and now!*

The truth is, we can't change everything overnight—nor should we. Any changes we make should be done one step at a time, each step covered with a liberal amount of prayer, conversation, and grace. Those little changes will add up to a big impact over time—and as a bonus, we won't be dragging a crew of whiplashed, burned out coleaders along with us!

Those in your circle of leadership likely aren't reading this book alongside you (although if they are, that's wonderful!). They might not be as intrigued as you are about the new information or ideas you discover in these pages. It's important to share what you're learning in simple, practical ways that are soaked in—you guessed it—grace.

At the end of each chapter, we conclude with three important questions. They will guide you through a process of celebration, contemplation, and action. Working through these questions will help prepare you to take your thoughts and learning to the rest of your team in positive, realistic, concrete ways.

So go ahead—dive into this resource with all the gusto of attending that next big conference! Just remember to bring your team along gently for the ride. Together, we know you'll make a big difference for vulnerable children and families in your community and around the world.

Community Guidelines

Here are a few helpful suggestions to guide your discussions as you bring any new information to your team. Some of the topics discussed may draw out deep emotional responses which require a healthy environment in order to be processed. Keeping these points in mind can help facilitate encouraging and thought-provoking dialogue for everyone.

- **Keep it small:** It can be best to introduce new ideas in smaller groups or meetings, rather than in a public setting.
- **Commit to confidentiality:** Any personal information or opinions shared in the meeting stays within that group.
- **Refrain from offering unsolicited advice:** Assume the role of encourager and discussion facilitator.
- **Use "I" statements rather than "you" or "we" statements:** This allows everyone's voice to be heard without making generalizations.
- **Leave room for everyone to speak:** Allow all to participate . . . but no one to dominate.
- **Avoid trying to give the "right" answers; focus more on giving "honest" answers:** Transparency will make your time richer and more effective.

Finding More Resources

Throughout the book, you will find resources for further exploration. All of these resources can be found online at missionwisebook.com. *We will continue to update this webpage with revised or additional resources as they become available, so bookmark the page and check back regularly!*

A PASTOR'S PERSPECTIVE

From One Church Leader to Another

I have had the privilege of serving as the missions pastor at Mosaic Church in Orlando, Florida, for more than a decade now. During that time, I've had the incredible opportunity to help develop and shape our theology, philosophy, and methodology when it comes to local and global missions.

Along the way, we have had to evaluate, rethink, and reimagine both how we engage our congregation in living on mission and how we come alongside ministry partners locally and globally to make the gospel known through church planting and works of justice and mercy. Some of our lessons learned have come from trial and error, learning as we go, making mistakes, and course correcting where needed. We have also been greatly helped by resources like *Generous Justice* by Tim Keller, *When Helping Hurts* by Steve Corbett and Brian Fikkert, and by the ministry and resources of the Christian Alliance for Orphans (CAFO). Participating in the annual CAFO Summit Conference has been a particularly invaluable experience for me as a missions pastor and for our leaders and volunteers at Mosaic.

When I first started attending Mosaic, it was a young church plant just beginning to grow into itself as a local church. Much of the ministry philosophy and methodology was still wet concrete. We were full of passion and zeal to "Love God, Love People, and Serve the World." We were convinced that God had called us to be a church that would be a part of "Changing the World." We preached that Jesus invites us to live on mission with Him and that His invitation to pick up our cross and follow Him is a call to participate with Him in redeeming unredeemed spaces in our world. For us that meant stepping into hard things for the sake of the gospel.

This really began to take shape in 2009 when our elders took a vision trip over to Ethiopia to explore opportunities to engage in the story in the northern Tigray region in the city of Axum. Our lead pastor returned from this trip and declared to our young church, "I'm not okay living in a world where parents have to make the choice between putting their children in an orphanage and letting them starve. I'm not okay with this, and we are going to do something about it!"

So we dove headfirst into a child sponsorship program in the city of Axum to try and do our best to help see "the orphans of today, become the leaders of tomorrow." We began sponsoring forty children classified as orphans by the local department of women and children. Over the next several years, this grew from forty children to one hundred children as well as helping with a water project and investing in the local hospital with equipment and training. We wanted to engage in the orphan crisis in Ethiopia with a holistic approach. We dreamed of seeing transformation in the city of Axum within ten years.

Yet looking back, while full of good intentions, our naive optimism is now laughable. We didn't know what we didn't know. And we had a lot of learning to do.

Simultaneously, many families in our church started fostering and adopting, including our lead pastor and his wife who adopted a sibling group of four from Ethiopia. As we got more involved in the world of "Orphan Care" we were introduced to resources like the Christian Alliance for Orphans, the annual CAFO summit, and Empowered to Connect. We were learning about things like trauma-informed care and wrap-around care as we sought to help our families who had adopted or were fostering and who were honestly drowning! All of this learning began to have an unexpected effect on our global missions efforts.

Throughout the years we've learned, adapted, and grown in our global missions efforts. We've had to modify partnerships, seek new partnerships, and even end old ones—all in an effort to be as wise and effective as possible. It has impacted how we invest financially in global efforts, how we conduct short-term mission trips and ultimately how and why we make the decisions we do to engage in various opportunities both around the world and right here in Orlando.

We've learned and stumbled over the years—but we've remained committed to stumbling forward with grace and to always be learning better and doing better along the way. And as we grow and learn we will continue to evaluate and shape our local and global missions philosophy and methodology accordingly.

Resources like this are invaluable to missions pastors and leaders like me. They not only bring clarity to questions I'm already asking but also help me identify new questions I didn't know I needed to be asking. But perhaps most importantly for us all is this—this book gives us the courage to ask the hard questions we know we need to be asking but for a variety of reasons have been trying to avoid. With an undertone of grace, empathy, and authority, you'll be confronted by some necessary truths but comforted by the assurance that you now have the resources and answers you need to make the decisions you need to make.

This short book will help you develop a local and global missions strategy that is ultimately beneficial to the children and families you desire to serve. It will help you as you evaluate current and new partnerships. It will help you as you seek to equip your church "to do justice, and to love kindness, and to walk humbly with your God" (Micah 6:8) as you engage in caring for orphans and vulnerable children globally around the world and locally right there in your own community. It will help you think holistically about how to actually serve children, families, and their communities well!

At Mosaic, we still want to be a part of changing the world. We want to see a world where the Church is mobilized and equipped to make the gospel known in word and deed. Where the global Church is known for moving toward the brokenness in our world, stepping into it to be redemptive with and for Jesus to the glory of God. And this resource will help us move closer to that vision!

—Gabriel Forsyth
Missions Pastor
Mosaic Church

1

A THEOLOGICAL BASIS FOR ORPHAN MINISTRY

The Gospel Is Our "Why"

Before we jump into the "whats" and "hows" of effective global engagement, let's start with the "why." What compels us as followers of Jesus, and as the Church collectively, to care for vulnerable children and families around the world?

Ultimately, we find our "why" in the gospel. The gospel acts as the grid through which all of God's work on our behalf is celebrated and all of our work on behalf of the vulnerable is demonstrated. Let's unpack that a little.

Doctrine of Adoption

One of the most prominent pieces of imagery running throughout Scripture depicting the character of God and His work on our behalf is the picture of family. Specifically, the illustration is rooted in the relationship between God as our Father and us as His dearly loved children.

> *"See what great love the Father has lavished on us, that we should be called children of God! And that we are!"*
> John 1:12-13 NIV

The hinge upon which this entire new relationship with God has been formed is beautifully illustrated in Scripture through the continuous use of the word "adoption."

"He predestined us for adoption to himself
as sons through Jesus Christ."
Ephesians 1:5

"You did not receive the spirit of slavery to fall
back into fear but you have received the Spirit of
adoption as sons, by whom we cry 'Abba! Father!'"
Romans 8:15

We were once outside the family of God but now, through the work of Christ on our behalf, have been adopted as dearly loved sons and daughters. We experience the rights and privileges of being known and loved as His! A new identity born out of a new way of how we relate to God—as our Father—and how He relates to us—as His children.

If our adoption into God's family is at the core of the gospel, then the gospel is certainly at the core of our calling to care for kids who need loving, safe, and permanent families to call their own. The gospel is also at the center of our calling to serve vulnerable families in any capacities available to ensure they are able to thrive together—healthy and whole.

The theology of our adoption helps form the basis of our "why." Why would we partner with organizations that promote the ethical placement of orphaned children into new forever families? Why would we partner with organizations that are committed to bringing systemic and sustainable renewal to families and communities? Because that's what Christ has done for us.

But it doesn't end there.

The truth is not all are called to adopt, nor is adoption always the necessary or right outcome to be pursued in the life of a vulnerable child. So how does this doctrine of adoption into the family of God practically translate into a message that might not include adoption as an application?

This is where a distinct, yet intricately intertwined understanding of the doctrine of "incarnation" can be incredibly helpful to press into as we form the theological motivations and articulations of our "why." It acts as a theological blanket, if you will, that can be laid out over us all under which implications and applications for everyone can be identified.

Doctrine of Incarnation

The word "incarnation" literally means to *assume human form*. The doctrine of Christ's incarnation speaks to God stepping into humanity, wrapping himself in flesh and living completely and fully as both God and man. It's most notably recognized at Christmas with the celebration of the birth of Jesus, yet its implications are far more pervasive than just the 25th of December every year.

> *"All this took place to fulfill what the Lord had said through the prophet: 'The virgin will conceive and give birth to a son, and they will call him Immanuel' (which means 'God with us')."*
> Matthew 1:22–23 NIV

At Christmas God effectively said, "I see you where you are and I'm coming after you!" He stepped out of His glory and into the fulness of our mess and brokenness as humanity. The incarnation reveals much about who God is and what God does. It tells us He is the kind of God who sees hard places and broken people and moves toward them, not away. He is "with us" in our failures, struggles, fears, and anxieties. He doesn't just get us through the mess and the pain of life—He walks with us in it. Jesus immersed Himself in our brokenness, carried our brokenness to the cross and was literally broken by our brokenness so that we don't have to be broken anymore. God saw our plight and moved toward us, not away from us. That is the good news of the gospel!

The apostle Paul reiterates the incarnation of Christ and beautifully ties it into God's redemptive pursuit of humanity to make us His children, when he writes:

> *"When the fullness of time had come, God sent forth his Son, born of woman, born under the law, to redeem those who were under the law, so that we might receive adoption as sons."*
>
> Galatians 4:4–5

Jesus was "born of woman" (incarnation) in order "that we might receive adoption" into His family. If the incarnation of Jesus is at the core of the gospel, then our stepping toward the hard and the broken is certainly at the core of our calling to care for the vulnerable.

The theology of Christ's incarnation helps form the basis of our "why." Why would we partner with organizations who through wise methods and informed best-practices immerse—or incarnate—themselves into hard and broken places? Why would we invest deeply into those places that are working toward hope and renewal in the lives of children, families and communities for the glory of God? Because that is what Christ has done for us.

The implications of the doctrine of incarnation are broad. The opportunities for each individual person to "incarnate" themselves into hard and broken places are endless and full of creativity—as are the opportunities to partner with organizations who do the same.

Frankly, this moves the conversation beyond just orphan care in some capacity—although this is a clear and vivid outlet to respond (as James 1:27 describes leaning into the lives of the vulnerable as one of the purest and most undeniable reflections of the gospel). Incarnation, however, speaks to a renewed posture and perspective toward the world around us in all matters of justice, mercy, and sacrifice.

The world says we should avoid hard and broken things, insulate ourselves from them and isolate our families from them. The gospel, however, suggests an entirely different posture and perspective. It compels us to "incarnate"—to step toward and wrap ourselves up in them. It invites us to not just "do" these things but instead to be these things—to become the kind of people who lean in toward and get involved with hard places and broken people around us—not step back, isolate, and insulate.

The gospel also changes the kinds of questions we ask ourselves. As we increasingly become more aware of what Jesus has done for us our questions begin to subtly and yet profoundly shift from things like, "Why would we do this?" to "In light of what Jesus has done for us, why would we *not*?" An entirely different question coming from an entirely different place—a question we seek for all who are engaged in this work to continually be asking and uniquely applying in their own journey toward caring for the most vulnerable among them and around them.

The opportunities to incarnate ourselves into hard and broken places are endless and full of diversity—and so too are our opportunities to partner with organizations who are meeting various types of need along the broader spectrum of caring for vulnerable children, families, and communities.

The application of incarnation in caring for vulnerable children and families is clear and undeniable—it is a beautifully powerful opportunity for us to see others in hard places and say to them, "I see you where you are and I'm coming after you."

Why do we work diligently as individuals, churches, and organizations to immerse ourselves and others into hard and broken places? Because that is exactly what Christ has done for us!

> *Adapted from* Everyone Can Do Something *by Jason Johnson (CAFO)*

WRAPPING UP AND MOVING FORWARD

Remember, there is so much grace here! As we know better, we can do better. If you're questioning the way you or your church has engaged in global missions in the past, remind yourself that you were doing the best you could within your circumstances. You didn't mess up; you showed up! And showing up is worth celebrating.

As we wrap up this chapter, consider:

- What's one way you or your church have "shown up" for children and families on the topics covered in this chapter? Take a moment to celebrate it!
- What's one thing you learned in this chapter that you feel compelled to share with the rest of your team?
- What's one practical next step you can take to make a small change based on your new knowledge or understanding? (This can be as simple as setting up a meeting with a stakeholder or reviewing one of the resources referenced in this book. Don't overcomplicate things or overburden yourself!)

2

THE POWER OF WORDS: WHO IS AN "ORPHAN"?

Saying What We Mean

It's easy to use the word "orphan" without truly understanding it. Many times we use it when referring to a vulnerable child. We may envision a young boy or girl whose parents have both died, leaving them alone in the world without a family to love and protect them. While orphans are certainly vulnerable, many vulnerable children are not true orphans at all.

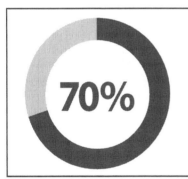

Approximately 70 percent of children living in children's homes or orphanages have at least one living biological parent.

Would it surprise you to know that around 70 percent of children living in children's homes or orphanages have at least one living biological parent?[1] These children are sometimes known as "social orphans." Of course, having a living parent does not necessarily mean a parent will be willing or able to care for a child. As an example, most children in the U.S. foster care system have living parents, but only a minority will return to live with their parents long-term.[2] Interestingly, children who have lost both biological parents are most frequently cared for by extended family.[3] This is often called kinship care.

The widely accepted definition of an orphan is a child under eighteen years of age who has lost one or both parents to any cause of death.[4] A child who has lost one of their biological parents is a single orphan; a child who has lost both of their biological parents is a double orphan.

Here's where confusion often occurs: using these definitions, many of the children we see photos of, hear stories about, and visit on our short-term missions, are either single orphans—*or not actually orphans at all.* When we hear statistics about the number of orphans around the world, it's important to ask ourselves how the terms are defined.

When you understand the problem, your church can more effectively be a part of the solution.

Why are so many children living in an orphanage or children's home if they have parents or family members who love them? There can be many reasons. The infographic on the right shows a few of the primary ones.

Often these reasons are interwoven and difficult to separate from one another. It's important to understand and have compassion for the challenging circumstances many families face, even as we seek to bring God's incarnational grace to them through the organizations we support.

It's also important to keep this context in mind when you hear orphan statistics. Why does all this matter to you as a mission leader? It matters because when you understand

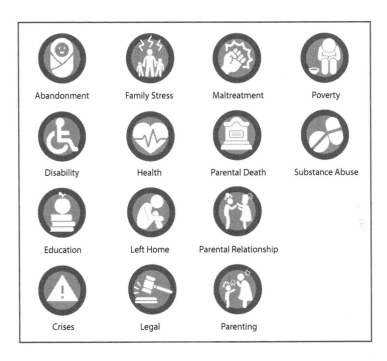

Abandonment   Family Stress   Maltreatment   Poverty

Disability   Health   Parental Death   Substance Abuse

Education   Left Home   Parental Relationship

Crises   Legal   Parenting

the problem, your church can more effectively be a part of the solution.

As a church, it's important to assess whether your partner organizations prioritize efforts to preserve struggling families and to reunify those that have been separated. Research suggests that children who are separated from their parents are much more vulnerable to a wide range of physical and emotional dangers.[5] The relational, physical, and spiritual support of the local church community are vital to helping these children thrive.

Understanding the terms we use helps to minimize confusion and maximize clarity as you evaluate programs or organizations to plug your church into—programs that are addressing the root causes of orphanhood. You and your congregation can be a part of placing children in families, just as the gospel models for us and compels us to do. Practically speaking, this might mean seeking out partnership opportunities with organizations that work closely through local churches that are actively working to keep children and families together in their communities by addressing the systemic issues that put them at risk.

Finally, not only do we need to define our terms and understand the underlying issues at play, but we also need to remember the distinct needs of each individual child. Scripture and science agree that children develop best in healthy, nurturing families. Organizations that do the best work in global orphan care are those that recognize seeking the best outcome for each child requires knowing much more than their orphan status alone; it requires knowing their status as a child of God, uniquely created by Him for His glory.

Meaning What We Say

If the word "orphan" is so easily misunderstood, why do we continue to use it?

Like many things in life, just because it can be difficult to understand, doesn't mean it's not important. The term "orphan," especially for followers of Jesus, helps us connect the needs of vulnerable children with the clear mandate in Scripture to protect and care for the "fatherless" and the "orphan."

At the same time, we should understand that the biblical concept of the "orphan" and "fatherless" includes more than just the boy or girl who has lost one or both parents. Rather, it describes the child who faces the world without the provision, protection, and nurture that parents uniquely provide. God calls His people to reflect His heart and character in choosing to "defend the cause of the fatherless," to "care for the orphan and widow in their distress," and to "set the lonely in families"— whatever the details of his or her situation may be.

In living out this high calling, it is our prayer to see the local church in every region increasingly play the central role in meeting the needs of orphans in distress—from family preservation and adoption; to provision for specific physical, social, emotional, and spiritual needs; to advocacy for government policies that combat systemic injustices.

For Western Christians, this includes a distinctive call to foster, mentor, and adopt children within our local foster systems as well as partner with and influence organizations addressing the global orphanage crisis with thoughtfulness, wise practices, and a focus on ensuring children are safe within the protective influence of a loving family.

Did You Know?

Most of the children in the U.S. foster care system still have living biological parents. Because of this, we tend not to use the word "orphan" when referring to children in foster care.

Equipped with this knowledge and understanding, your church can play a vital supportive role globally— humbly aiding local churches and ministries that serve with excellence. Ultimately, our final hope is this: that Christians in every nation will rise as the primary answer to the needs of the orphans in their midst, glorifying God as a reflection of His great love for the orphan and for us.

If you want to learn more about how to accurately understand and share global orphan statistics, check out CAFO's booklet, On Understanding Orphan Statistics, *online at* missionwisebook.com.

WRAPPING UP AND MOVING FORWARD

Remember, there is so much grace here! As we know better, we can do better. If you're questioning the way you or your church has engaged in global missions in the past, remind yourself that you were doing the best you could within your circumstances. You didn't mess up; you showed up! And showing up is worth celebrating.

As we wrap up this chapter, consider:

- What's one way you or your church have "shown up" for children and families on the topics covered in this chapter? Take a moment to celebrate it!
- What's one thing you learned in this chapter that you feel compelled to share with the rest of your team?
- What's one practical next step you can take to make a small change based on your new knowledge or understanding? (This can be as simple as setting up a meeting with a stakeholder or reviewing one of the resources referenced in this book. Don't overcomplicate things or overburden yourself!)

3

HELPING CHILDREN FULFILL THEIR POTENTIAL

You might be tempted to skip over this chapter and get to the "real" substance of this book—partnership. Why is it important for a pastor or missions leader to understand child development? What does it have to do with global missions?

It matters because the call of the church is to bring God's healing, incarnational grace to a broken and hurting world. Sin has permeated every part of life on earth—including our physical, emotional, and social development. Orphans and vulnerable children have experienced this brokenness in tangible, often devastating ways that significantly impact their development.

However, by God's design, we are hardwired for hope! The human capacity for resilience and healing is incredible. Understanding some foundational concepts of child development will help you to:

1. **Acknowledge** and celebrate God's amazing design, as well as lament where sin has caused brokenness;
2. **Understand** how the church can best address this brokenness in a way that aligns with what Scripture and science tell us; and
3. **Evaluate** current and future partnerships to make sure you can support the way they address children's needs and developmental struggles.

Taking the time to understand these basic ideas will provide a framework and a scaffolding for your ministry to orphans and vulnerable children for years to come.

Developing the Way God Intended

We serve an incredible Creator who has designed us to develop in uniquely creative yet cohesive ways. Child development refers to the sequence of physical, language, thought, and emotional changes that occur in a child from birth to the beginning of adulthood. It is influenced both by nature (genetics) and nurture (environment).

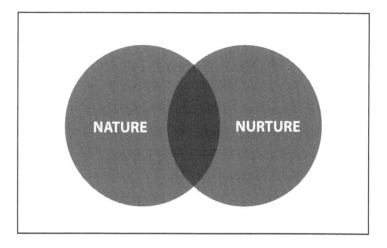

These two factors contribute to the holistic development of a child that allows them to experience full human flourishing the way God intended. While we cannot control most of the "nature" factors, we can (and should) make sure a child has the healthiest "nurture" possible.

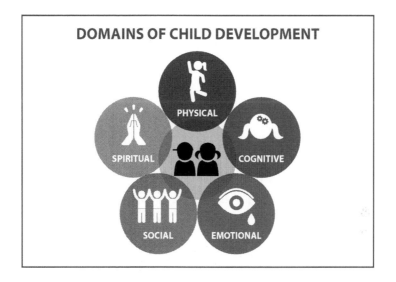

For example, a loving caregiver can help a child to trust and develop a framework for healthy relationships. Having safe space to run and play can help a child's physical development. Healthy food leads to better nutrition and healthier bodies. Reading books to a child helps them develop a good vocabulary.

When those physical and emotional needs are met, a child is able to be open and receptive to their spiritual needs—allowing us to share the gospel in a powerful way. However, when those needs are not met, it can negatively impact not only their physical and emotional development, but their spiritual development as well.

When the World is Broken: How Does Trauma Impact Child Development?

One of the most profound, negative impacts on any human being is trauma. Trauma is any deeply distressing or disturbing experience. This could be abuse, the death of a loved one, or a natural disaster. Everyone experiences trauma differently; if it's deeply distressing to you, then it will impact you as a traumatic experience, regardless of how others may experience the same event or circumstance.

Trauma is a clear expression of the fall. It can be acute (a single stressful event), chronic (repeated or prolonged exposure to highly stressful events), or complex (exposure to multiple traumatic events). According to the Harvard Center on the Developing Child,[6] a child's stress response can also be described by three categories: positive, tolerable, or toxic.[7]

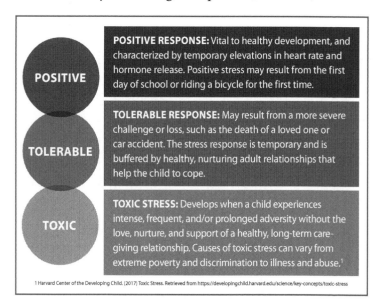

POSITIVE RESPONSE: Vital to healthy development, and characterized by temporary elevations in heart rate and hormone release. Positive stress may result from the first day of school or riding a bicycle for the first time.

TOLERABLE RESPONSE: May result from a more severe challenge or loss, such as the death of a loved one or car accident. The stress response is temporary and is buffered by healthy, nurturing adult relationships that help the child to cope.

TOXIC STRESS: Develops when a child experiences intense, frequent, and/or prolonged adversity without the love, nurture, and support of a healthy, long-term caregiving relationship. Causes of toxic stress can vary from extreme poverty and discrimination to illness and abuse.[1]

POSITIVE

TOLERABLE

TOXIC

1 Harvard Center of the Developing Child. (2017) Toxic Stress. Retrieved from https://developingchild.harvard.edu/science/key-concepts/toxic-stress

When a child experiences toxic stress, trauma, or adversity, their brain functioning is not *damaged*, but rather may *develop abnormally*. They may experience emotional, behavioral, or physical health problems.

The good news is that it's possible to actually reverse some of the negative effects of trauma. Our brain structure and function can literally be changed by changing the input it receives. This is called *neuroplasticity*. The primary way this happens is through safe, nurturing relationships.

As followers of Jesus, this shouldn't surprise us! All of Scripture reveals that healing comes through relationships. Our ultimate, eternal healing can only occur through our relationship with God. He pursued us and opened the door for us to return His love in a small measure. Not only does healing come through relationships, but so does our proper functioning and ultimate thriving. We've been created for relationship—each one of us placed within the body of Christ not just to perform a specific function, but to also understand our need for and interdependence upon being connected to others.[8]

In a similar way, children who've experienced trauma experience healing growth through relationships. God has wired us this way! When a child is given a supportive environment from parents, caregivers, teachers, and their community, their brains have a chance to redirect—literally become reshaped—toward normal development. It is a physical manifestation of renewing our minds.[9]

This is the awesome power of neuroplasticity and a reflection of the gospel at work in the physical world. We'll explore this idea in more depth later, but for now, we can marvel in our Creator's intricate design of our bodies and brains.

If you want to learn more about child development, check out CAFO's free e-course, Child Development, *online at* missionwisebook.com.

ACEs Aren't Just for Cards

As you speak with nonprofits and individuals who serve vulnerable children, you may hear them use the acronym, "ACEs." ACEs stands for Adverse Childhood Experiences—or traumas.

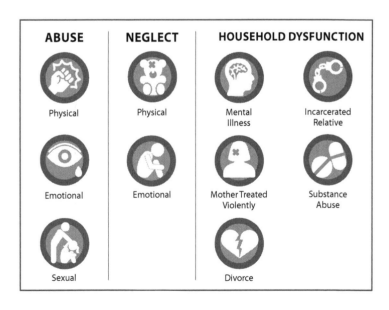

ABUSE	NEGLECT	HOUSEHOLD DYSFUNCTION	
Physical	Physical	Mental Illness	Incarcerated Relative
Emotional	Emotional	Mother Treated Violently	Substance Abuse
Sexual		Divorce	

There are ten main types of ACEs[10] which researchers and professionals use to understand a child's history.[11] However, ACEs can occur in categories beyond these (such as the loss of a parent).

As the number of ACEs increases, so does the risk of health problems, emotional disorders, substance abuse, and high-risk behaviors.[12]

What many parents and caregivers of vulnerable children do not know, however, is the impact an attachment figure can have on improving a child's development.[13] Although unhealthy caregiver relationships can serve as a source of toxic stress, healthy relationships with a caregiver may contribute to a child's ability to overcome hardship.

> *If you want to learn more about neuroplasticity, check out the CAFO's short booklet,* The Changing Brain: Created to Heal, *online at* missionwisebook.com.
>
> *If you want to learn more about ACEs, check out the Ted Talk by Nadine Burke Harris, "How Childhood Trauma Affects Health Across a Lifetime" also available online at* missionwisebook.com.

Attachment and Resilience:
How Relationships Can Heal

"We are biologically hardwired to crave connection."

Attachment After Adversity: Building Resilience through Relationship

For children, attachment is the emotional bond that develops as a stable caregiver consistently meets the child's needs and comforts the child during times of distress. If a child cries and is met with tender care, food, or a clean diaper, they begin to internalize the message, "I am worthy. I am important. My needs will be met." When those needs are not met, they hear the opposite message: "I'm unworthy. I'm not important. My needs won't be met."

Attachment has profound effects not only on a child's body and brain, but also on their soul.

Attachment has profound effects not only on a child's body and brain, but also on their soul.[14] Their attachment with a parent or caregiver creates the framework for how that child views all relationships, including his or her relationship with God.

As a church, we should care about attachment not just because it impacts the well-being of a child of God, but more importantly because it has eternal consequences. Helping a child establish secure attachments will set them up to receive the good news of the gospel and the love of their heavenly Father[15] with greater clarity and receptiveness. They will have seen, felt and grown to trust physically that which we are praying they receive spiritually—a God who is close to them in their distress and who offers love, renewal, and hope.

How does healthy attachment form? Over thousands of interactions with a specific caregiver. They cry, we answer; they reach, we answer; they babble, we answer. The key here is *consistency*.

This attachment figure is then supported by a network of individuals (i.e., a significant other, grandparents, siblings, a community) who are vital in building an attachment network with the infant. Understanding this process will be key in our conversation on short-term missions later.

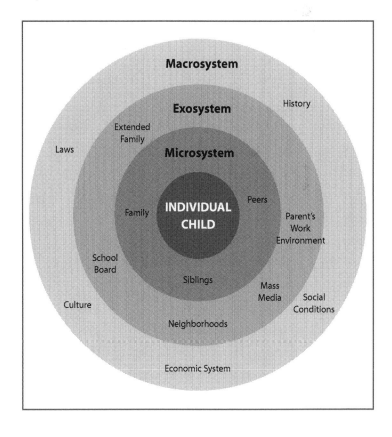

Unfortunately, orphans or vulnerable children may have experienced unhealthy relationships that lead to less-than-optimal attachments to their caregivers.[16] However, there is hope!

> *"Losing a healthy, long-term caregiver may be part of the problem, but gaining one can be part of the solution."*
> Attachment + Resilience

Healthy relationships can be built, even with nonbiological caregivers.[17] This healthy attachment can be a key ingredient to help a child bounce back after adversity. When a caregiver connects with a child and provides a healthy, supportive caregiving environment, they support the development of resilience.[18]

Like development, resilience is formed through a combination of nature and nurture. Some children are naturally more resilient, but all children do better with the right support surrounding them. A child with secure attachment to their caregiver has a strong network of support to help them navigate the challenges that trauma brings.

Understanding how attachment through consistency forms, we may consider evaluating how staff, house parents, and residential caregivers are utilized within the programs we are partnering with and helping to fund. Are they providing the consistency and stability children need to truly form strong, healthy attachments? Or is it a rotating system of shift workers tasked with certain duties that run paramount to actually ensuring children are thriving in strong relational contexts with caregivers?

Like attachment, resilience has a direct impact on a child's soul. In Christ we are "more than conquerors" (Romans 8:37). Scripture is full of promises that the Lord will be our strength and our shield, going before us and behind us in every circumstance of our lives. Understanding resilience can help us see God at work in the lives of orphaned and vulnerable children, and we in turn can help them understand this profound truth. Our partnerships can then be built on and motivated by the incredible hope of God's current work and future redemption in the lives of these precious children!

If you want to learn more about attachment for children from hard places, check out CAFO's booklet, Building Resilience through Relationship, *online at* missionwisebook.com.

WRAPPING UP AND MOVING FORWARD

Remember, there is so much grace here! As we know better, we can do better. If you're questioning the way you or your church has engaged in global missions in the past, remind yourself that you were doing the best you could within your circumstances. You didn't mess up; you showed up! And showing up is worth celebrating.

As we wrap up this chapter, consider:

- What's one way you or your church have "shown up" for children and families on the topics covered in this chapter? Take a moment to celebrate it!
- What's one thing you learned in this chapter that you feel compelled to share with the rest of your team?
- What's one practical next step you can take to make a small change based on your new knowledge or understanding? (This can be as simple as setting up a meeting with a stakeholder or reviewing one of the resources referenced in this book. Don't overcomplicate things or overburden yourself!)

A PASTOR'S PERSPECTIVE

Relationships That Heal

Three weeks of serving at an orphanage in Guatemala City were ending, and goodbyes were in process on the side of a lush mountain that sixty-five children had found refuge and safety at a small, family-style children's home. Our University Missions Team was quite large; twenty-five of us had landed with little more than broken Spanish and a heart to serve as an offering to this beautiful home and its children, but we had so much faith that God would use our time for something good. As students loaded the bus I noticed the smallest of the children, a sweet three-year-old boy, sitting on a bench, head down, tears streaming down his face. As I approached, he looked up, and said, "You will never come back, people like you never do."

Over the course of the next twelve years this little boy would encounter over six thousand visitors and would be parented by more than thirty house parents (by his count). People would come, and people would go—visitors, teachers, caregivers, and even other children. They all had one thing in common: they did not stay. This is the story for so many children who experience residential care around the world. As we zoom the lens out and look not at one moment, age, or stage but at the fifteen-year journey of this one boy, we gain an opportunity to ask pivotal questions that can, if we are both humble and intentional, lead to dramatic shifts in how we engage globally.

Words like "trauma" and "attachment" were not a part of our vocabulary twenty years ago and they certainly did not inform the way we engaged vulnerable children and families around the world. We don't know what we don't know, and so we did the best we could with the knowledge at hand. Today, we have access to so many relevant resources to help shape and inform our practices.

As you have learned in this chapter, understanding trauma, attachment, and child development is essential to creating a healthy environment where children can learn and grow physically, emotionally, and relationally.

Traditionally, our church, Houston's First Baptist Church, has partnered missionally with those who serve orphaned and vulnerable children around the world, providing basic needs like food, water, consistent education, access to good medical care as well as safe housing. All these things are important for sure, but what we've learned in the past 10 years has led us to rethink literally everything in regard to engagement. It has motivated us to dig deeper, beyond meeting short-term basic needs, and toward the cultivation of environments that lend to long-term relational healing.

Through phenomenal educational opportunities with Trauma Free World, Empowered to Connect and the work of The Karyn Purvis Institute for Child Development we have been able to learn and apply powerful, healing principles. Equipping our church staff and lay leaders on the basics of trauma, attachment, and child development has become an essential to ministry. Simultaneously we've begun to lean into our global partners, listening and learning and meeting them where they are. Many of them have begun to request training and equipping opportunities, allowing us to cultivate an environment of mutual learning.

One of the most powerful things we learned was that trauma changes the brain, body, biology, beliefs, and behavior of a person. At times, we've felt overwhelmed by this knowledge but when we understand the profound impact of trauma, it can reframe our perceptions and hopefully our actions. We have found that ruptures caused by trauma become places of deep spiritual battles. Knowing this has changed the way we pray, relate and engage gospel-centered conversations.

We learned that attachment matters! In fact, research tells us the most pivotal attachment building happens in the first 365 days of a child's life and when a child has a lack of consistency in primary caregivers, they can develop indiscriminate attachment. We realized our encounters with children had been unhealthy and our engagements were largely on our "terms." We needed to step back, do more listening, adjust expectations, and put our partners in the driver's seat. We needed to listen to the voices of those serving in the field full-time, to adults who grew up in the protective system and even children.

Over the last five years we have become learners. This has meant training for staff across all campuses and auxiliary ministries at our church, intense training for mission's teams and even the development of an OVC Care Team made up of members dedicated to learning, praying and advocating. It's led to honoring caregivers and staff both locally and globally so that attachment can be cultivated without interruption.

Additionally, we learned that we are "hardwired for connection" and that development of the brain happens through consistent mentoring. All along we wanted to be a part of creating environments that were safe for children to develop, play and grow but again, but we just didn't know enough. We had looked for good adult-to-child ratios with our partners, but realized that just as important was the health and longevity of the caregivers serving children. As a result, it has become incredibly important for us to ensure that partners and their staff are healthy and remain consistent, cultivating attachment and sensory-rich, healing environments.

He held out his hand, tears still streaming and dropped a perfect pink flower into my hand. "Please come back. Will you?" God's grace was with us in that moment of uncertainty as we wept together. I did come back and continue to be a part of his life today. These years have taught us that we may not know what tomorrow holds, but we can trust God with it!

What we didn't know 22 years ago, the children we served knew by experience. Attachment matters. A heartbreaking conversation became a profound and powerful lesson that has caused us to place a deep value on protecting, valuing and cultivating attachment-rich environments for orphaned and vulnerable children. This young man, now all grown up with a wife and three beautiful children of his own, continues to have a powerful voice in our midst.

May we continue to listen to the children, allowing them to push us as the Church to grow deeper in knowledge and understanding, to empower more intentional, consistent relationships and to demonstrate wild generosity!

—Toni Lynn Steere
Director of Legacy 68:5
Houston's First Baptist Church

4

QUALITY CARE
IN GLOBAL
MISSIONS

Better Than Nothing? Confronting the Lies

We've already recognized *why* we are called to care for orphans and vulnerable children: the gospel compels us to act out of love and obedience to God, through the doctrines of adoption and incarnation. However, in our desire to obey this call, it can be tempting to jump into an exciting prospective partnership without fully understanding the *how*—the quality of care the organization provides. Why does this matter?

Maybe your church financially supports an orphanage overseas. You fundraised for the building, and now your congregation is deeply invested in sponsoring the children who live there. You're beginning to believe that it would be better for those children to be in a family, but isn't an orphanage better than living on the streets?

Perhaps your church regularly coordinates food drives to supply a food pantry at a local elementary school. Much of the food is canned or boxed, with limited nutritional value; but isn't it better than seeing children go hungry?

Or you may partner with a large sponsorship organization to provide education for children who otherwise couldn't afford school fees. Because of the scale of the program, classes are overcrowded and teachers struggle to provide individualized support to students. The teachers also don't have access to adequate training or support themselves. But at least the children are in a classroom . . . right?

Your church may have had the opportunity to partner with a nonprofit to build a well in a rural community, bringing fresh water to the families who live there. However, three years later, you visit the site to find that the well has broken down, and no one in the community had the tools or training to fix it. It has sat empty and rusted for over a year—but wasn't it better than leaving a community without life-giving water, even if only for a short time?

You may have coordinated a clothing drive for a local foster care closet or an upcoming mission trip. Some of the clothing is old and worn out . . . but isn't it better than nothing at all?

Or perhaps a group of high school students in your church collected and donated backpacks for children in foster care. Unbeknownst to you, the agency already has hundreds of backpacks from donations last year just sitting in a storage closet taking up space—but they're afraid to say no to a church that wants to do something for them and the children they serve, so they smile and accept the gift. Isn't something practical like a backpack, even if it's not their most pressing need, better than nothing?

Whether we are serving children in our own city or around the world, it can be easy to convince ourselves that *something* is better than *nothing*.

Now we're by no means suggesting that your church has ever bought into the "better than nothing" mentality! It was most likely the other church down the street, right? They're always doing stuff like that . . . but not us! Or maybe if we took an honest assessment, we might find some examples in our own ministry at times as well. We've all been there—fallen victim to the "better than nothing" mentality and unintentionally victimized others with it. It's all part of learning and growing and getting better, which is our goal here.

Learning and growing doesn't mean that we must understand everything perfectly, or find the perfect partner, to begin serving orphans and vulnerable children at all. It simply means that we refuse to settle for "better than nothing" when God calls us to so much more. When we know better, we can do better.

Many organizations have wonderful hearts, and many more are doing incredible work around the world. All of us want to make decisions based on the best interest of children that will allow them to fulfill their God-given potential. Yet not all nonprofits have the support or understanding to implement best practices as they serve children.

> *Many organizations have wonderful hearts, and many more are doing incredible work around the world.*

As a ministry leader, you have a unique position of influence. This is where you and your church can make a tremendous difference! When you understand the dynamics of child development and best practices in global missions, you can support and encourage organizations to continue improving the quality of care they provide. Where improvements need to be made, you can be the organization's champion. Where they are excelling in their care, you can be their encouragement. And in all aspects, you can be praying for them in the good work they strive to do.

That's right, you don't just have to partner with organizations *as is*; you can actually be an agent of growth and change for your partners as well. As a matter of fact, many global organizations long for deeper levels of partnership beyond just financial support, the supplying of goods, or sponsoring children. They desire the deeper things as well that come through relationship—things like leadership development, access to some of the best and most current research on child development and best-practices for orphan care. These are things we, in the Western church, are generally able to access far more easily than are our partners on the ground in developing countries. Consider your current partnerships: how might you begin to help them grow in the good work they are already trying to do? In what ways can your partnerships take on that new relational level of coach, mentor, and advocate?

For a moment, think of your own child or a child you love dearly. If your child were separated from parental care, how would you want them to be cared for? If your child's family was experiencing extreme poverty, how would you want others to serve them? If your child were in the situation of the children served by the program you partner with, would you be pleased with the way they would be cared for? Are there ways you can help them grow in these things?

We believe every child, every human, is created with *imago dei*—the image of God—stamped on them. Because of this, we are called to serve them with excellence as far as we are able. That is the perspective we must fight for as we keep moving forward.

Best Practice: Buzzwords or Building Blocks?

If we're not careful, *best practice* can become a buzzword—the missional equivalent of the classic Sunday school answer, "Jesus!" In reality, best practice encompasses many different ideas. All of them are nuanced, and they evolve as the research helps us continue to learn how we can know better and do better. Think of it as the theology of your mission work—it doesn't make you love God in and of itself (that's the work of the Spirit), but used properly, it can help you love and understand Him in a deeper way. Best practice doesn't solve every problem, but it does help us practically live out our call to provide compassionate, high-quality care to those we serve.

At CAFO, we've developed a self-assessment tool for organizations to help them reflect, learn, and grow in key areas of best practice. While you certainly don't need to be experts in these areas, it can be helpful to have a working knowledge of them so that you can have deeper conversations with your partners as you seek to learn and grow together. Rather than seeing these topics as trendy buzzwords, we can understand them as building blocks that help organizations establish a solid foundation from which healthy and thriving ministry flows.

So what are these building blocks—the core elements of a healthy organization?

FISCAL ACCOUNTABILITY. Good stewardship and ethical financial practices are critical to organizational longevity and wellbeing.

GOOD GOVERNANCE. A healthy and engaged board will provide guidance, oversight, and support to the mission of an organization.

CODE OF CONDUCT. A clearly defined code of conduct outlines the expectations, responsibilities, and proper practices for staff and volunteers.

CASE MANAGEMENT. All placements, including family reintegration, require thorough assessment, training, and follow-up support by professionalized staff to ensure child welfare and protection.

QUALIFIED STAFF. Qualified staff possess both the technical skills and community knowledge to effectively fulfill their position and to support the mission of the organization.

MONITORING AND EVALUATION. Monitoring and Evaluation (M&E) is a process that helps improve performance and achieve results. Its goal is to improve current and future management of outputs, outcomes and impact. Employing monitoring and evaluation practices ensures adequate progress toward an organization's intended outcomes.

CHILD PROTECTION. Proactively safeguarding children from harm is first priority.

CONFIDENTIALITY. Measures are taken to protect the confidentiality of all children and families served.

CHILD FOCUS. Care decisions are on a case-by-case basis in order to ensure the child's health, safety, security, and long-term well-being.

SPIRITUAL DEVELOPMENT. Wise spiritual instruction and guidance—including freedom to question and seek—help a child form a foundational sense of their value, identity, and purpose as beings created in God's image and loved by Him.

CONTINUITY OF CARE. Long-term health of vulnerable children takes priority over short-term success.

PARTNERSHIP. Healthy and strategic partnerships maximize the impact of any OVC—serving organization. Learning from and working with other organizations allows for better quality of services.

LOCAL EMPOWERMENT. The primary role of western organizations serving cross-culturally is to empower local involvement in caring for OVC.

GATEKEEPING. Good gatekeeping establishes processes for decision-making that ensure children receive alternative care only when necessary, and that children and families receive the supports that are in their best interest.

CHILD DEVELOPMENT. Every child has the God-given right to healthy physical, spiritual, educational, emotional, and social development.

SPECIAL NEEDS. Children with learning difficulties, physical disability, or emotional and behavioral challenges require programming suited to their needs.

FAMILY STRENGTHENING. Actively engaging in, or partnering with organizations that engage in, services that support families staying intact is a foundational component for any organization that seeks to support vulnerable children.

REINTEGRATION. Reintegration into the family and community is a long-term process, requiring great care to assess and support the health of a family.

ALTERNATIVE FAMILY CARE. Both the Bible and social science affirm that the ideal environment for children is a safe, permanent family. When not possible for a child to live with biological family, an alternative family placement like adoption or foster care is preferable.

RESIDENTIAL CARE. If all family placements have been explored and residential care is deemed necessary, it should be as small, and family-like as possible, and organized around the rights of the child.

SHORT-TERM VOLUNTEERING. Short-term missions and visions trips carry with them the potential for both great good and tremendous harm, especially when we hope to benefit children.

We will dive a bit deeper into some of these topics in the next few chapters, but as you can see, there are quite a few! Supporting your partners as they learn and grow in these areas will be an incredible blessing—to them, to you, and to the children you serve together.

Several of these core elements refer to the importance of family-based care. In the last few years, there has been a growing movement that emphasizes the value (some would say necessity) of family in the life of a child. It's here that we turn next.

If you want to learn more about each of these core elements of best practice, check out CAFO's interactive booklet, The Core Elements: Companion Primer. *For further resources on each topic, check out the accompanying toolkit,* Core Elements of Success in OVC Care. *Both of these resources can be found online at* missionwisebook.com.

WRAPPING UP AND MOVING FORWARD

Remember, there is so much grace here! As we know better, we can do better. If you're questioning the way you or your church has engaged in global missions in the past, remind yourself that you were doing the best you could within your circumstances. You didn't mess up; you showed up! And showing up is worth celebrating.

As we wrap up this chapter, consider:
- What's one way you or your church have "shown up" for children and families on the topics covered in this chapter? Take a moment to celebrate it!
- What's one thing you learned in this chapter that you feel compelled to share with the rest of your team?
- What's one practical next step you can take to make a small change based on your new knowledge or understanding? (This can be as simple as setting up a meeting with a stakeholder or reviewing one of the resources referenced in this book. Don't overcomplicate things or overburden yourself!)

5

WE ARE FAMILY

Scripture and Science Agree—
Children Need Families

Scripture[19] and academic research[20] both reveal that children develop best in families. God designed the family as a primary source of the love, protection, guidance, and structure children need to thrive. And the impact continues far beyond childhood! Being a part of a healthy family provides a lifelong sense of belonging and connection and sets the stage for stepping into new roles as parents and community members in adulthood.

However, we live in a broken world and not all biological parents are healthy or capable of caring for their children. In some instances, parents may need support to parent successfully, or it may be necessary to remove the child from parental care for their safety and well-being.

Within the global church, there is a growing movement that recognizes the importance of family in the life of every child and strives to ensure that children are cared for within families, rather than in residential care, orphanages, children's homes, or other live-in facilities.

This movement is well rooted in Scripture. As we've seen, God calls us to have compassion, understanding, commitment, and care for the fatherless and the widowed,[21] and puts forth a special call to care for vulnerable children in both word and deed.[22] However, in almost all instances, the Bible talks about protecting widows and fatherless children not as two separate categories but as one unit—as a family.

Why is family so important? Our family relationships often mirror our relationship with God. A healthy family can nurture spiritual learning and formation. This biblical call to care for orphans, partnered with the theological framework of God's intentions for family, can inspire us to care for all God's children within the context of families. By doing so, we are showing them a mirror of God's love for them.

So . . . if a healthy family is the ideal place for a child to grow, then how do we understand all the orphanages and residential care centers around the world? Remember the idea that *something* is better than *nothing*? This can be a motivating reason for continuing to support residential care for vulnerable children, even if we'd rather see them in families.

The truth is, residential care can have its place. In *some* situations, for a *short period of time*, residential care might be helpful for *specific* older children. For example, a teenage girl who's been trafficked might benefit from some time in a therapeutic group home that specializes in trauma recovery, so that she can begin to heal and prepare for life in a family. An adolescent boy who has been living on the streets may require support and intervention prior to being ready to live in a family setting.

However, if God intends for children to grow best in a family, then residential care should never be the only (or first) option for a struggling family. One way we can help keep children in families is by making sure that residential care is always placed within the context of other care options. We'll take a look at that process in the next section.

It's also important to remember that many of the children in residential care are not truly orphans.[23,24,25] Poverty is one of the top reasons they are not living with their families.[26] Parents often place them into care so they can have access to food, education, or other opportunities— mistakenly believing that their child will be better off living apart from them.

Research shows us that this simply isn't the case[27] and requires us to ask some questions about our church's global partnership strategy. Is your current scope of partnership and engagement unintentionally reinforcing a system that is ultimately not ideal for children in the long term? Are there ways in which you can continue to support the residential facility, help them grow and adapt so children thrive in a more family-like setting *and* begin to address some of the systemic reasons children are there in the first place? These can be things like poverty, lack of education, or lack of access to basic healthcare.

A PASTOR'S PERSPECTIVE

We are fortunate to have forty-year veteran missionaries in Kenya who have taught us the disturbing supply-demand reality of orphanages. In Kenya, many parents are made to believe (especially when times get hard) that Western-backed orphanages will provide the brightest future for their children. These children are recruited, separated from their families, and raised in artificial environments that, while possibly "safe," deprive them of critical social and cultural identity, as well as basic nurture. When they turn eighteen they have no way of reintegrating into society. In collectivist cultures this is the equivalent of death. Thus, most live in even deeper poverty thereafter. Most of us don't stick around long enough to watch the rest of the story. When our compassion stops at quick fixes, we can fail to consider the long-term impacts of our actions.

—**Aaron**
Pastor

Many nonprofit staff and researchers are becoming concerned with the struggles children experience as they grow up in residential care settings. Some of those struggles include isolation, loss of a sense of belonging, identity struggles, and difficulty maintaining connections as they grow. There are also long-term negative impacts on physical and mental growth and development. The younger children are when they enter care, and the longer they stay, the stronger the impact. Even the best group homes simply can't provide everything a family can.

Yet as we've seen in each topic so far—in Christ, there is always hope. Becoming part of a family, even after living in residential care, can be a healing experience.[28] The love, nurture, stability, and connection of a family can literally rewire their brain! Knowing this causes excitement to stir in our spirit, as we contemplate the ways our church can support the efforts of our partners to provide this healing opportunity to children in need.

Caring Well from A to Z: A Continuum of Care

We've seen the importance of family in the life of any child— especially those who are orphaned or vulnerable. However, we also know that each child's situation is unique, and family isn't always an immediate possibility for them. Sometimes families are unhealthy or ill-equipped to provide the kind of care their children need.

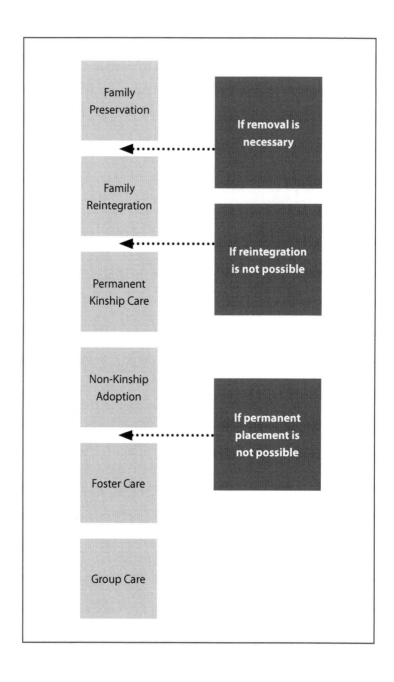

That's why it's important for any service provider to have a range of options available when they look at the needs of each child. The official term for this range of options is a *continuum of care*.

Picture it like a long line, with family preservation on one side and residential care on the other. In between, there are a spectrum of options that may be necessary, either temporarily or long-term, before a child is able to be reunited with their family or placed in a new one.

While a child is experiencing this continuum of care, it's important for the families to receive support and resources as well. No matter what option a child experiences along the continuum of care, they are experiencing it because they are also experiencing other risk factors. They need additional support in order to heal and thrive—support that your partners, or their partners, are hopefully able to provide.

Making sure children and families have the support and resources they need for their particular situation requires an investment of relationship over time. In the same way your relationship with church members allows you to know on a deeper level what internal and external barriers they are facing in their walk with the Lord, so your partners' relationship with the children and families they serve will allow them (and you) to understand the internal and external barriers they face in their goal of remaining healthy and intact.

> **A Reminder**
>
> *Keep in mind that no single organization will be able to provide all of these options on their own. Strong partnership among organizations is the key to making all these options available—with excellence—to children and families in need. If you want to learn more about how to support your partner as they build a continuum of care by forging partnerships in their region, check out CAFO's free e-course on Community Mapping & Partnership, available online at* missionwisebook.com.

With all this in mind, let's take a quick look at the different options along the continuum of care.

Family Preservation: This is our first choice whenever it is possible and safe! It includes providing resources (such as food, educational fees, or shelter) and support (such as parenting or business training) that allow families in poverty or crisis to remain together. Removing children from their families can be disruptive, traumatic, and have long-lasting negative effects, so we want to avoid it whenever possible.

If a family must be separated, they may walk through a series of other care options, hopefully ending in family reintegration.

Family Reintegration: This is the process of transitioning a child back to his or her biological family after they've been separated. It is not a one-time event but rather an ongoing process of surrounding the family with the support and resources they need to thrive. It's especially important for nonprofit staff to understand and address the root cause of the initial separation before a child returns home. In both family preservation and family reintegration, monitoring and support are key.

Consider

Maria and Jose are still living with their single father since their mother passed away two years ago. When the pandemic hit, their father lost his job and didn't have enough money to buy laptops or tablets for Maria and Jose to join their classes online. Their teacher was concerned when they didn't show up for online school and shared this information with local child welfare authorities. They wanted to remove Maria and Jose from their home and place them in foster care. Distraught, their father called a local nonprofit and asked for help. After listening to his needs, nonprofit staff were able to get refurbished laptops for the children, as well as help their father find a new job at the local grocery store. Not only that, but they check on the family weekly and connect them with local resources that meet additional needs—from counseling to nutritious meals to math tutoring for Jose. They are invested in making sure this family stays together!

Before family reunification is possible (or when it is not), child welfare professionals will begin exploring other options. Often, their first choice is to pursue kinship care.

Kinship Care: When immediate family cannot care for a child, a close relative (such as a grandparent, aunt, or older sibling) may step forward. This is the most common type of care for orphans and vulnerable children around the world.[29] Extended families have the benefit of keeping a child connected to their community, family, and culture—but often they receive little attention or support from outside sources. Wrap-around support is crucial in these situations, and may be a way your church can support your partners in their work.

Consider

James lives in Kenya. For most of his childhood, he lived with his single mother. She owned a small shop in their village, selling groceries and other basic necessities. However, when he was twelve years old, his mother got very sick and died. One of his aunts, who helped his mother run the shop, brought James to live with them. While food is sometimes limited, he is able to stay in his community, surrounded by those he loves. He continues to attend school with his cousins and work at the shop in the afternoons, where he has many memories of spending time with his mother.

If kinship care is not available, the next step is often foster care or adoption.

Foster Care: Although foster care varies widely around the world, it is usually some type of full-time care provided by a nonrelated individual or family. Formal foster care is often overseen by the government, although nonprofits and churches often play key roles in recruiting and training families and supporting children in care. Informal foster care may occur when a child is placed with someone like a trusted neighbor or community member. In either situation, foster care can be temporary or permanent.

Adoption: When children have no possibility of safely remaining with family or relatives, adoption is often the next best option to provide a stable, loving family. Like many aspects of orphan care, adoption is beautiful and complex and should be approached with lots of learning and prayer.

Another option for young adults at this point is supported independent living.

Supported Independent Living: For some young adults, such as those who age out of the foster care system, supported independent living allows them to continue receiving support as they launch into adulthood. Organizations may assist them with housing (including basic household items like dishes or bedding), education, mentorship, career planning, and more.

Consider

Amy is seventeen years old. She has been in the foster care system for five years and will age out in just a few months. She lives in an apartment with several other young adults, overseen by regular visits from their social worker. With the support of her guidance counselor, Amy decides to finish her high school education at a local community college. Her guidance counselor connects her with an organization that helps her find and apply for scholarships so she can pursue this dream. They also connect her with a local church that is passionate about supporting teens who age out of the foster care system. One of the families in that church wants to build a relationship with Amy. She sits with them at church and comes home with them every Sunday afternoon for lunch. She is welcome to stop by any night of the week to join them for dinner, throw a load of laundry in their washer, or ask for help with her homework. When Amy receives good news about one of her scholarship applications, they are the first people she calls! With the support of the organization and her church family, Amy moves into adulthood with the resources she needs to thrive.

In certain situations, especially where foster care and adoption are not viable options, children end up experiencing residential care.

Residential Care: As we discussed earlier in this book, residential care includes orphanages, children's homes, and other group homes. Contrary to popular belief, they exist in the United States as well, although they are less common.

> ### Consider
> Mari lives in India. When she was just five years old, her parents died in a taxi accident. Mari ended up living on the streets and was sold into sex trafficking. When she was finally rescued at age twelve, she spent time in a residential care facility designed for girls who have had these experiences. The staff spent time helping Mari and the other girls process through their trauma and find healing. When she was ready, the staff helped Mari find a permanent family who adopted her. While she still misses her parents and continues to heal from her past experiences, Mari has the support of a loving and supportive family where she belongs.

Each option has its place and is a piece of the puzzle that is global orphan care. However, one challenge can be the tendency to immediately jump to residential care when families are struggling, particularly outside the U.S. This is something we must all prayerfully wrestle through.

One question we can ask ourselves as we partner with those who are serving children through any form of alternative care is this: **If my child were separated from my**

care, would this place be my first choice or my last resort for their care? If we honestly answer this question, it will go a long way in helping us embrace the importance of these various care options.

As we wrap up this section, consider this encouraging fact: residential care centers are often uniquely well-equipped to transition into family support centers. While the process is complex and requires some initial funding, it ultimately enables organizations to provide more services at a lower cost—all while keeping families together. Residential care centers aren't a barrier to best practice. They can actually be a key part of the solution!

In a recent survey,[30] many organizations reported that one of the biggest barriers to their transition to family-based care was fear of losing support from key stakeholders. If you partner with an organization that prioritizes residential care, this can be an exciting way to engage with them. Your support can make all the difference. If you'd like to learn more about this process, check out one of the sections in the appendix in this book titled, *Going Deeper: Transitioning to Family-Based Care.*

Now that we have a basic understanding of each option along the continuum of care, we can also appreciate that caring for vulnerable children is more complex than we might imagine. We cannot see their plight without also seeing the systems around them: families, communities, and cultures with unique strengths and challenges.

God calls us to see the world holistically and serve accordingly. Part of this call includes working to empower local people, who are experts in their own communities, to implement local solutions.

> *If you want to learn more about the continuum of care, check out Faith to Action's booklet,* A Continuum of Care, *online at* faithtoaction.org/a-continuum-of-care.
>
> *If you want to learn more about how a child's attachment is impacted by each of these care options, check out CAFO's booklet,* Attachment After Adversity, *online at* missionwisebook.com.

Local People, Local Solutions

Each of us is an expert in our own experience. This is also true of our partners around the world! They know their communities and their culture far better than we ever will. They are already in positions of leadership in those spaces, and our respect for those positions will help our partnerships be exponentially more effective.

There are often strong emotional attachments to certain types of care—both for organizations and the churches who support them. While it's important to continually learn and grow, and it is certainly acceptable to have conversations with your partners about the ways their programs are designed and implemented, all of this should be done with a heart of humility for their expertise. The primary role of the Church as we serve cross-culturally should be to empower local involvement as they care for orphans and vulnerable children.

We want to communicate with our local partners about what their hopes and dreams are for the children in their care and then help them achieve those dreams. We want the biggest part of our partnership to be learning from our partners and allowing them to drive the vision and seek the solutions that fit best in their context. This is why local leadership (both on the ground and in the offices and boardrooms) is so important.

Listening well and asking good questions communicates that we honor and respect our partners beyond their ability to help us meet our ministry goals. Why do they do things the way that they do? What have been the barriers to improvement that they've experienced? Perhaps they've simply been waiting for a church with the vision and funding to support them in it! We will only achieve lasting change by honoring and supporting their unique perspectives, experiences, authority and connections.

One way to grow and stretch our partnerships is to be mindful of the way we ask for our partner's input. Where we may tend to ask them, "What do you think about this program or solution?" rephrasing our question to ask, "What do you see as a viable program or solution in this situation?" can change the conversation entirely. Submitting to our partner's wisdom and experience within their local context can be game changing—not only for them, as they realize that we are truly there to serve their needs, but also for us, as we are able to witness and participate in their vision for those they serve.

The challenges our partners face are often systemic and intergenerational. They won't be solved quickly, and the nuances very often cannot be understood by those of us who are outsiders in their culture or community. Recognizing these facts with humility can open up the door to honest conversations with your partners, where they feel free to express their frustrations and hopes.

Case Studies

Organization A: This organization works with young girls in Cambodia who are at risk of being trafficked. While a majority of the staff on the ground are Cambodian, most of the leadership isn't local. In fact, the main office is in the United States, and all of the board members live there as well. Because Cambodian culture tends to be more indirect than American culture, the Cambodian staff often feel a power differential between themselves and the leadership that keeps them from sharing their thoughts and perspectives freely. There are several important practices that they would like to change, based on their local knowledge and experience. However, the leadership has never asked for their input, and there has never been space for them to share.

> *Organization B:* *This organization works in Zimbabwe, working with young girls at risk of child marriages. While there are a few staff members in the United States, a majority of the staff and leadership are native Zimbabweans. They are the ones shaping the policy and budget decisions, and they are able to adapt and adjust those decisions in real time as they see the impact of their work. The U.S. staff are there to support the vision cast by local leadership and to offer insight when invited to do so. The work is collaborative, but the Zimbabwean leadership knows that the U.S. staff respect their role and will honor their goals for the organization.*

By empowering local people to implement local solutions, we are unleashing a powerful force for lasting systemic change that will far outlast your church's involvement. Wouldn't that be something to celebrate?

The next chapter will share some practical tips for supporting local empowerment. Before we get there, let's consider what work needs to be done on our end to prepare us for those conversations.

> *If you want to learn more about empowerment from local leaders themselves, take a look at CAFO's booklet,* Engaging Local Cultures, *online at* missionwisebook.com.

Good Intentions Are Not Enough: Knowing Better to Doing Better

"Every child has the God-given right to healthy physical, spiritual, educational, emotional, and social development."

Core Elements Primer

In the same way that *something* isn't always better than *nothing*, so good intentions cannot replace best practice as we care for orphans and vulnerable children. As a leader, you likely know this all too well! We are all well-intentioned people in a way, looking at other well-intentioned people in the pews around us and wondering who will volunteer first, give more, or start that ministry that the community so desperately needs. Intentions are only impactful when they inspire action. Knowing better must lead to doing better!

It's worth repeating: As a missions pastor (or someone who helps your church or organization make decisions about where to focus and with whom you will partner externally) you have a unique position of influence in this space. Your support and input hold weight within the organizations you support, especially if you have a deep relationship of faithful partnership over the years. As you learn more about best practices, don't be afraid to have open, honest, and humble conversations with those partners. The goal of this book is to help you feel equipped in these conversations and interested in learning more.

Actively partnering with organizations that engage in helping families stay intact is a foundational component for any church that seeks to support vulnerable children. As we learn about the basic concepts of child development, trauma, attachment, and resilience, it informs and inspires our partnerships, as it transforms the way we see orphan care.

We begin to value organizations that make care decisions on a case-by-case basis in order to ensure the child's health, safety, security, and long-term well-being. We prioritize children's long-term health over interventions that may feel like a short-term success. We seek out strategic partnerships that maximize their impact and collaborate with others to provide the best care possible. Above all, we live out our call to serve the orphan and the widow in a more holistic way, helping children form a foundational sense of their value, identity, and purpose as beings created in God's image and loved by Him.

If you want to learn more about the importance of family-based care, check out CAFO's booklet, Moving Towards Family Solutions, *online at* missionwisebook.com; *or Faith to Action's booklet,* Transitioning to Family Care for Children, *online at* faithtoaction.org/transitioning-to-care-for-children.

Making the Best of a Broken Reality

Our quest to provide the best care possible for orphans and vulnerable children will always be hindered by the sin and brokenness that pervades our world. Until Christ comes again and renews all things, we will be fighting a spiritual battle as we seek to answer His call.

However, that shouldn't stop us from seeking to make the best out of a broken reality. We cannot allow discouragement or lack of understanding to prevent us from thinking critically about the way we approach our mission partnerships in this area.

All children have the right to receive care in a way that best suits their needs. For most children, this will hopefully be in a family setting—either through biological family, kinship care, adoption, or foster care. For others it may look a bit differently, in the context of small, family-like group care. Care decisions must be made based on what fosters a child's short- and long-term well-being, rather than what is easiest for programs, caregivers, and those who fund them. No child should be in residential care simply because it is the only option available or because that type of program is more conducive to soliciting donor dollars.

Where family options don't exist, it should be part of the church's mission to help develop them. As we consider how we can best achieve this goal, here are a few concepts to consider.

1. **Consider unintended consequences of making care available.** Starting (or even maintaining) residential care programs can have unintended consequences. In many communities, sending a child to the local residential care center can be seen as an easy answer to lack of resources. Having an alternative care option available may lead families to place their child in care unnecessarily. We need to do everything we can to prevent this from happening.

2. **Excellent gatekeeping is vital.** Gatekeeping is the decision-making process to prevent unnecessary family separation and to ensure a care plan that is in the best interests of the child when separation does occur. It helps make sure that children receive other forms of care only when necessary and that children and families receive the support they need to stay together whenever possible.

3. **Good residential care is difficult.** For contexts where residential care is the only available option, it may seem simpler to continue that model and do it really well, rather than considering other care models. However, residential care should never be the default option. It is extremely difficult, time-intensive, and expensive to do well. We've also seen the negative impacts it has on child development. Organizations should only operate small group care as a last resort and only with the necessary funding, staff, and

support to meet the needs of the few children who will be best served by family-like group care.

4. **Size is not the only factor in determining quality of care.** Large institutional housing is never the answer. Big group homes with high child-to-staff ratios are the most detrimental form of care. However, it is also entirely possible to have institutional, impersonal care in a small group setting as well. Quality matters!

5. **All care should look as much like family as possible.** What every child needs most is the love, belonging, and protection that comes most naturally from living in families. When other types of care are necessary, they should look as close to a family as possible. Moving children between rooms, homes, and caregivers is not healthy or appropriate for their development, nor is having too many children in the home. Relationships between children and caregivers should be as stable and long-term as possible, ideally extending well beyond graduation from the program.

6. **Children need to be part of the community.** Children who live their life on a compound, going to school, eating meals, and working and playing within a very limited and controlled environment will likely struggle as they transition to living independently in their community. It is vital that all children be given the opportunity to

regularly connect with adults and children outside the residential care center, to worship, to attend school, and to participate in local community life.

7. **Children should be prepared for independent living when they reach adulthood.** Eventually, every child will become an adult, and one of the most important ways to love them well is to ensure they are equipped for independence. The test of whether a program is successful is not whether a child is happy or getting good grades, but rather whether they are able to tackle adulthood successfully, holding a job, maintaining healthy relationships, and eventually raising their own children well.

8. **Understand the difference between transitional and permanent care.** In some cases, small group care is needed temporarily. This can include emergency situations such as separation from parental care in natural disasters, parental illness, or political displacement. Sometimes, transitional care may be needed to prepare a child for family care, such as in the case of children who have been living on the streets or trafficked reintegrating with their families. Access to high-quality short-term care is vital, but organizations must use good gatekeeping and case management to ensure those children in need of temporary care don't end up in long-term residential care.

9.   **Build capacity to build families and communities.**
     In some situations, residential care providers are the
     ideal fit to provide community services that prevent
     unnecessary separation of children from families.
     Opening up chairs in a school to community children,
     providing daycare or after-school care, or offering
     counseling services to families at risk are all ways
     residential care providers can repurpose current
     resources to be part of keeping families together.

These are some very big ideas that will take much
prayer and conversation to explore with your ministry team
and partners. The next chapter will dive into the nitty-gritty
process of having those conversations and evaluating your
partnerships in light of all the information you've learned so
far. For now, use these points as a springboard for prayer,
deep thought, and perhaps even journaling if that's your
thing! However you do it, take some time to explore how
God may want to challenge our traditional view of orphan
care and begin making the best of our broken reality.

*Adapted from the CAFO article, "12 Principles on the
Place for High-Quality Residential Care and How We
Achieve It". If you want to learn more about some of
the ideas presented here, take a look at Faith to Action's
booklet,* Children, Orphanages, and Families, *online at
faithtoaction.org/children-orphanages-and-families.*

A Note about Grace

If this is your first time hearing about many of these ideas, now is the time for grace!

It can be easy to feel discouraged at our previous lack of understanding or overwhelmed at our next steps. We might grieve the ways we were involved with orphan care before we knew some of these concepts. However, we can't allow conviction to turn into condemnation.

On the first day we know better, we are able to do better. It's important to give ourselves, our churches, and our partners grace for the past—and to write a "grace check" for the future! As long as we are striving to honor the Lord with our partnerships, He will be in them. He will direct our steps and honor our desire to serve His children with excellence.

This process is not a one-time event but a journey of continually knowing better so that we can do better. And it's a journey that we're on together! We hope you have a community—whether that's CAFO or another group—cheering you on and working alongside you to better serve children and families . . . together.

WRAPPING UP AND MOVING FORWARD

Remember, there is so much grace here! As we know better, we can do better. If you're questioning the way you or your church has engaged in global missions in the past, remind yourself that you were doing the best you could within your circumstances. You didn't mess up; you showed up! And showing up is worth celebrating.

As we wrap up this chapter, consider:

- What's one way you or your church have "shown up" for children and families on the topics covered in this chapter? Take a moment to celebrate it!
- What's one thing you learned in this chapter that you feel compelled to share with the rest of your team?
- What's one practical next step you can take to make a small change based on your new knowledge or understanding? (This can be as simple as setting up a meeting with a stakeholder or reviewing one of the resources referenced in this book. Don't overcomplicate things or overburden yourself!)

6

HOW NOW SHALL WE SERVE?

Forming and Maintaining Strategic Partnerships

Your church needs more than just your church to effectively engage in the mission of God around the world. Identifying, vetting and formalizing strategic partnerships with organizations is a vital and necessary component of not only your global engagement strategy, but of your overall missions and outreach initiatives as a church.

Now that you have a deeper understanding of best practices in serving orphans and vulnerable children, the challenge is to weave that knowledge into your global missions framework. As high-quality orphan care becomes a part of your core values in mission work, it will become easier and easier to incorporate it into your everyday conversations and decision-making processes. In the beginning, however, don't make any hasty decisions. The best thing you can do is start where you are.

Start Where You Are

First, take a look inward. As a church, and as a pastoral team, now is a great time to get clear on your own aims and objectives for global engagement. How does what you've learned impact your vision for the future? Take some time to pray and discuss these ideas.

This process is best done in community! If you have several people on your missions team, schedule a time to go through it together; if not, ask some of the other pastors to read this book and join you in the process. The more your team is on the same page at this stage, the better it will be as you move forward.

Next, take a look at your current partnerships. Where have you been investing? This doesn't just mean monetarily, although that is certainly part of it. Where have your church members been volunteering their time? What organizations have you taken short-term missions teams through? Who do you have deep, long-term relationships with?

These two steps—meeting with your team and taking inventory of your current partnerships—may take some time to do thoroughly, but they are well worth the effort. Not only do they help you clarify your thoughts, but they also reveal where you may have gaps in your understanding of your partner's programs or questions they can answer. Note, we're not suggesting that you identify who your current partnerships are and immediately scrap them if they aren't operating according to the best of the best practices we've been discussing in this book. Instead, we're inviting you to consider where some gaps might exist that are fixable and solvable and how your church, in continued partnership with the agency or organization, might be able to learn and grow together.

Once you've looked inward at your own vision and assessed your current partnerships, the next step is to evaluate the kind of healthy, strategic partner you'd like to become.

Mutuality, Not Dependency

What does the word "partner" actually mean? The dictionary defines it as *a person or group that takes part with another or others in doing something.* Throughout Scripture, we are called to partner with God in His glorious work of redemption on earth. We take part in what He is doing. We can also partner with one another—a powerful way to engage with other image bearers who may be different from us in many ways, and yet share a mutual love for the Lord and a desire to serve Him.

When we partner with the organizations who serve orphans and vulnerable children, we are coming alongside them in the good work that they are already doing. We are not replacing them or redirecting them; we are not there to achieve our own goals or have beautiful photos to put on our website. We are taking part in the mission God has called them to.

Because of this, partnership looks much different than simple charity. It is longer, more in-depth, and it relies heavily on relationships. It doesn't breed dependency. It is mutually beneficial for both parties, avoiding the danger of shame and stigmatization that comes when we slip into a savior mentality. It goes beyond financial support to prayer, mentorship, and encouragement—flowing both directions. Engaging in a partnership means staying aware of power dynamics, cultural differences, and our own internal motivations, and submitting those to the power of the gospel at work in our own heart and in the places where our partners live.

What Are Power Dynamics?

Power dynamics are simply the way power is distributed within a relationship. This can be related to financial or material means, or it can be related to spiritual or relational authority.

For example, your church might be investing thousands of dollars into a partner's work overseas. You may then decide you want to take a group from the church on a mission trip to go work at one of their ministry sites. However, they may not have the capacity to host you or the need for you to come at this time. Or, if they were honest, perhaps having a team from your church there will actually cost them greatly—in staff time, energy, and focus that could otherwise be best directed toward the children and families in the community they are serving. However, they're afraid to tell you no. Why? Because you sit in the seat of power. You represent funding, and they may not want to upset you in fear that it might jeopardize that financial relationship. So, they say, "Yes, you can come," knowing it's not what is best at the time.

It's important to be aware of how both we and our partners perceive the power dynamics within our relationship, and to consider how that might impact communication, trust, transparency, and mutuality.

Different cultures also define and perceive power differently. A statement we as Westerners might admire as "assertive" may feel like a power play to those from less confrontational cultures.

Power isn't inherently good or bad, but it can be used for either good or bad purposes—even unintentionally! Staying aware of the power dynamics at play in our partnerships can help us better communicate our support with humility and curiosity.

Mutuality means radical honesty and shared responsibility. It looks like open conversations about where your support is most helpful—and where it might unintentionally be harmful. It fosters a sense of respect and dignity between you and your partner.

How can we develop a mindset of mutuality as we serve our partners? We commit to examining our partnerships deeply and committing to them fully, so that we can intentionally learn and grow within the context of relationships. We go deep instead of wide.

To learn more about how Scripture guides us to partner with God and others in this work, take a look at Loom International's worksheet, titled "Tools and Strategies for Restoration," in the appendix of this book.

Deep, Not Wide

Now that we've evaluated our current partnerships, and determined what kind of partner we'd like to become, we're ready to engage with others.

As leaders who have a heart for people, we often try to take on the weight of the world. If we're not careful, our rallying cry may echo Paul's: "I have become all things to all people, that by all means I might save some,"[31] without holding it in balance with Jesus' words: "Whatever you did for you of the least of these . . . , you did for me."[32]

In this global age, where we are more interconnected than ever before, there are countless opportunities for partnership. Your email inbox is likely full of inquiries from countless nonprofits who would love to receive financial and spiritual support from you. Name a country, a project, or a topic you are passionate about, and there are dozens of organizations who would be the "perfect fit"! While evaluating your current partnerships is relatively simple, choosing new partnerships can feel incredibly overwhelming.

In general, it is better to have fewer partners with deeper relationships, rather than a large number of partners whom you only know superficially.

In general, it is better to have fewer partners with deeper relationships, rather than a large number of partners whom you only know superficially.

The exact number will depend on the size of your church and your staff's capacity, but going deeper rather than wider in your partnerships will allow you to intentionally cultivate the mutuality, trust, and understanding you desire.

Our ultimate goal is to accomplish more together than we could apart. Healthy, strategic partnerships allow us to come alongside those who are doing the good work and propel them forward with the resources God has entrusted to us. So how do we assess the health of our partnerships? Let's get practical.

Nuts and Bolts: The Practical Steps of Evaluating Partnerships

When we see ourselves and our church as part of a larger whole, it's good motivation to step into healthy, life-giving partnerships. Evaluating partnerships requires a willingness to ask questions and a curiosity that allows us to seek answers with humility.

When you evaluate a new partnership or a new project with a current partner, there are several questions that can provide clarification. Asking these questions can help both parties understand the potential risks and benefits, as well as each side's role in the partnership. Ideally, this process should be reciprocal—involving both partners having open and honest dialogue.

For New Partners

Assessing the fit of a **new** partnership typically involves three steps:

- Asking a series of basic questions
- Initiating a shorter-term project, with time limits
- Partnering in a longer-term, more involved project

Each of these stages includes a time of assessment, with the opportunity to decide not to pursue the partnership.

When assessing whether a potential partnership is a good fit, we want to start with several basic questions.

- **Is the potential partner legally registered?** We want to ensure any potential partners are registered with the appropriate local, regional, and national authorities. If not, why not? Are they willing to become registered? If not, why not?

- **Would our collaboration be beneficial to the children and families they serve?** How would children and families benefit? Is the partnership foremost about their good?

- **Does our potential partner adhere to a Child Protection Policy?** It is appropriate to ask to review their policy. Avoiding harm to children is paramount to all work with vulnerable children and families. (If you want to learn more about the ins and outs of a Child

Protection Policy, check out CAFO's Child Protection e-course, available online at *missionwisebook.com.*)

- **Does our potential partner know their aims?** Do they have a mission statement, vision statement, and objectives?

- **Does our potential partner have accountability in place?** Do they have a board or other governing body? How are they accountable for finances? How are they accountable for program goals and objectives? How are they accountable to donors?

- **Does the internet reveal anything alarming?** The internet can be a valuable tool for learning information a potential partner might not provide. Learning about the program, staff, and board from a website may provide insights. Reviewing social media accounts of the program or key leaders may inform the questions you want to ask.

- **How do they represent their work and the people they serve?** Ask to be on their communication list, and follow the program on social media. Do they represent their work honestly? Do they represent the people they serve with dignity?

- **Do multiple people from our organization believe this partnership is a good idea?** Is only one person

leading the charge? Is there consensus among our
leadership?

• **What references do they have?** Do you have any
contacts in common whom you could talk with? Can
you speak to another partner to learn more about their
experience? What is their reputation in their local
community?

It's important to take the time as a leadership team to
develop the questions that best capture the intersection of
your church's mission and the broader scope of best practice
in orphan care. This can be a relatively simple process and
can smooth the way for future partnerships.

**Some additional questions to consider when
evaluating a potential partner:**

• *Is their style of leadership one we can respect and honor?*
• *Will we, can we, or should we be their primary funder?*
• *Do we share similar missions and goals?*
• *What is their understanding of best practice (in
attachment, child development, family preservation,
etc.), and does it align with what we believe Scripture
and science teach?*
• *Will our partnership provide mutual benefit? Rather
than simply answering "yes" or "no," take some time
to list out the benefits on each side. Are they balanced,
not just in number but in weight and impact?*

Working together on one small project can be a great first step. It will allow those involved to see whether the relationship is a good fit. If it is, engaging in progressively longer-term or more involved projects can build the partnership. Building trust takes consistent character and quality across time, and the process cannot be rushed.

Practices that lead to healthy partnerships:
- *Cultivating transparency*
- *Listening, listening, listening*
- *Clarifying expectations*
- *Developing a shared vision that breeds trust*
- *Setting shared goals*
- *Establishing accountability*
- *Encouraging radical ownership on both sides*
- *Prioritizing open and honest communication*
- *Practicing humility*
- *Saturating the relationship in prayer*

For Current Partners

You may be wondering about assessing fit in the partnerships you already have. Although this process is simplest prior to committing to a partnership, it is never too late to consider whether the partnership is a fit. Walking through the steps above with current partners can serve as a jumping-off point for meaningful and clarifying conversations with them.

You may find that a current partner is not a good fit. In such situations, there are two options:

1.   Influence toward change
2.   End the partnership

We strongly encourage not dropping a partnership too quickly, without having extensive conversations. It has the potential to create significant amounts of collateral damage. For example, if you are funding a residential home (i.e., orphanage) and your support helps to feed the children, then immediately dropping partnership and ceasing your funding could significantly impact those children and their daily needs.

In some cases, it may be possible to work with a partner to make changes that would make them a better fit. For example, if they are not legally registered, you may be able to support them in that process. In these cases, the time you invest to support your partner may multiply your impact by leading to better care for the children and families they serve.

Sometimes, our partners may long to make changes in their program but lack enough support and funding to do so. They may fear that their partners (us!) will withdraw their support if they change. They may have creative solutions they've been dreaming about, if only someone would encourage them to release those dreams and take action. This is why open and honest communication is vital.

In other situations, a partner may not be open to making changes. Or you may find you have fundamentally different goals, and it is not possible for the relationship to be mutually beneficial. In these cases, it is appropriate and even advisable to find effective ways to end the partnership. If possible, it is ideal to maintain positive regard for one another. It can be as simple as saying,

> *"We respect you and your organization. One key priority for us is that our partners will _____. We understand that is not a priority for you at this time. Therefore, we will no longer be able to partner in an official capacity, although we hope to stay connected. We look forward to seeing how God continues to work through your program."*

These conversations can be difficult, but remember, you are making thoughtful decisions that will best serve the best interest of the children and families you serve together.

A PASTOR'S PERSPECTIVE

As we were learning more about how to best care for orphans and vulnerable children, we began to evaluate our partnership with the child sponsorship program in Axum, Ethiopia. While our hope was to remain in partnership with one another while working to influence change, the program directors ultimately resisted. We knew we were in danger of doing more harm than good if we continued in this partnership. It became clear that our only other option was to move on.

This was such a difficult decision as we wondered about the one hundred children we were sponsoring and what would happen to them. But in the end, we had to trust God, that He is sovereign and He is ultimately the Father of the fatherless and protector of widows and He settles the solitary in a home (Psalm 68:5–6).

Thankfully, we were able to find another like-minded partnership in the same region that we were able to engage with, and we continue to partner with them today.

—Gabriel Forsyth
Missions Pastor
Mosaic Church, Winter Garden, Florida

Above all, throughout the process of evaluation, it's important to keep the main thing the main thing. Prayer is the most powerful tool in your evaluation toolbox! The Holy Spirit will give wisdom when you ask (James 1:5), and God will be faithful to honor your heart when you seek to follow His guidance with your current and future partners.

> *Adapted from CAFO's free training module,* Community Mapping & Partnership, *available online at* missionwisebook.com. *For further resources, check out CAFO Church Ministries' booklet,* Global Engagement and the Church.

Three Keys of Healthy Partnership

Before we wrap up this chapter, let's zoom out a bit and look at an ideal partnership. While no partnership is perfect, there are three key ingredients that every healthy partnership has in common. Intentionally taking these three action steps will help you improve even the best partnerships, taking them to the next level.

1. **Cultivate mutual respect.** Although partnerships are ultimately about creating greater impact for the children and families our partners serve, they should also be healthy for each party involved. Without intentionality, partnerships can quickly become unequal

or even exploitative. Especially when partnerships cross cultures, and when the partnership includes the exchange of money, there can be a tendency for one partner to dominate the relationship (for more on this dynamic, check out the book *When Helping Hurts* by Brian Fikkert and Steve Corbett).

Have you heard the story about the mouse and the elephant? It's a cautionary tale of the dangers of inequality in partnership.

The Elephant and the Mouse

An elephant and a mouse were best friends. One day, they decided to throw a party. They invited all of their animal friends and together, they all talked and laughed and danced the night away. No one laughed harder or danced faster than the elephant—he was thrilled to celebrate with his best friend. At the end of the night, as everyone started to go home, the elephant began calling for the mouse, hoping to share the joy of the night. The mouse didn't answer. The elephant began looking for the elephant and soon noticed the mouse at his feet . . . lifeless.

If we don't exercise caution, we can become so excited about what we believe is good and right that we harm our partner.

Case Study

A young American volunteer went to West Africa to serve alongside a local missionary. The missionary had been working with the local church, focusing on increasing awareness of the need for evangelism and spreading God's Word across the whole globe. They learned from a local pastor that, as a result of that teaching, the church's annual missions budget had grown from forty-five dollars to sixty-one dollars. They were so excited that the church, with that money, decided to plant another church in order to reach more people and share the gospel more widely. The young volunteer shared in their excitement, but was disheartened by the seemingly small budget. Wanting to help them in their mission to evangelize, she made a huge donation—$6,800—to help them build the new church building. While incredibly generous, the gift was detrimental to the local church because the pastor lost sight of the church's focus and began to seek out more funding from more donors, rather than rejoicing in the sacrificial giving of his own church community. Meanwhile, the missionary was devastated as he saw his efforts at promoting self-support in the local church go down the drain.

Even unhealthy partnerships can come from good intentions. If the young missionary had taken on the role of a learner rather than a rescuer, a mutual partnership of equals may have emerged. Allowing a partnership to evolve slowly, with plenty of time for listening and understanding, will lead to more secure and sustainable relationships in the long term.

2.   **Communicate expectations.** Each program and individual will have their own expectations, whether they are aware of them or not. If not communicated properly, expectations can go unmet and lead to resentment and conflict. The results of such situations can hinder the ability to serve vulnerable children and families.

Outlining expectations in writing is one key to the success of your partnership relationship. Some expectations may be more logistical in nature (such as those in an agreement template), and some may be more interpersonal (such as those outlined in the CAFO Fostering Trust in Collaboration Agreement, available online at *missionwisebook.com*). Depending on the type of relationship, your partner may already have those documents available. However, your program may need to draft your own document for other partnerships.

Each partnership agreement should include:

- Who is involved?
- What are the goals?
- Who are we intending to benefit?
- What are the expectations of each program?
- How will we approach decision making?
- How will we revise procedures (if necessary)?
- How will fundraising and financial assets be managed?

- How will we represent and discuss our partnership with outside individuals?
- What parameters need to be put in place?
- How often will we meet to monitor progress and collaborate?
- How will we attribute results?
- How and how often will we evaluate the health of this partnership?
- If and when the partnership ends, how will that be done?

Keep in mind that every program is different, so tweaks and adjustments to a partnership document should be expected.

3. **Reflect regularly.** Like any relationship, there will be change across time in partnership. Partners may grow or shrink, may shift their focus, may have a change in leadership, or experience many other adjustments. Although this is completely normal, it may lead to the partnership functioning differently or even becoming obsolete or unproductive over time. Therefore, it is important to reflect and reevaluate whether the partnership continues to be valuable and effective. Utilizing a tool like the Partnership Review Template (p. 51, from the Partnering Initiative, available online at *missionwisebook.com*) on an annual basis can assist you and your partners in having regular check-ins to evaluate whether the partnership continues to better

serve the people we are trying to care for. Further, if changes need to be made regarding the partnership, these conversations provide an excellent opportunity to discuss and agree to adjustments in a proactive manner.

As with all relationships, a partnership cannot be reduced down to a formula for success. But these three ingredients—respect, communication, and reflection—will go a long way in building strong, thriving relationships.

When Helping Helps

The point of this chapter is not to discourage or overwhelm you with a massive overhaul of your missions program. Nor is it a prescription for constant critique of your current partnerships. The goal is actually to encourage and equip you!

If we don't understand child development or the importance of a family, we can unknowingly cause harm through our partnerships. But the opposite is also true! Knowing these facts can help us approach our partnerships with eyes wide open—with a heart *and* a mind ready to engage in providing the best care possible for children in need.

As our approach shifts, our impact shifts as well. Instead of simply feeding hungry children, we are increasing the capacity of the local church to meet both physical and spiritual needs. Rather than supporting the same residential program year after year, we begin to see children placed into loving, permanent families—until the residential homes become thriving community centers! This is the difference between providing short-term relief—which at times will be a temporary necessity in the face of things like natural disasters and medical outbreaks—and long-term community development.

Through development, our goal becomes serving the community through our local partners and addressing systemic issues for long-term empowerment and sustainability. Success comes when we're no longer needed in the same capacity over time. When children are separated from families, it doesn't just affect one person—it has a generational ripple effect. However, the same is true when we see children returned to a family. The impact will be exponentially greater than we can ask or imagine!

The work you put into evaluating your partnerships and having honest conversations with your partners will pay off many times over as you grow into deeper and richer relationships with them to accomplish this. And while we're never done learning, the process will become easier over time until it's second nature. You and your church can feel confident that, with God's help, you are not settling for *good enough* but truly seeking *the best it can be.*

WRAPPING UP AND MOVING FORWARD

Remember, there is so much grace here! As we know better, we can do better. If you're questioning the way you or your church has engaged in global missions in the past, remind yourself that you were doing the best you could within your circumstances. You didn't mess up; you showed up! And showing up is worth celebrating.

As we wrap up this chapter, consider:

- What's one way you or your church have "shown up" for children and families on the topics covered in this chapter? Take a moment to celebrate it!
- What's one thing you learned in this chapter that you feel compelled to share with the rest of your team?
- What's one practical next step you can take to make a small change based on your new knowledge or understanding? (This can be as simple as setting up a meeting with a stakeholder or reviewing one of the resources referenced in this book. Don't overcomplicate things or overburden yourself!)

A PASTOR'S PERSPECTIVE

Rethinking Partnership

The DNA of Port City Community Church has been infused with care for the orphan from the beginning. Our church was planted in 1999, and by 2004, we had jumped with both feet into pioneering a new ministry in Kenya that supported children living on the streets. Over the next decade, we sent dozens of teams, hundreds of participants, and millions of dollars to support a long-term group home and later, a private school.

We began a sponsorship program to raise support to send the children through school and onto further education. Sponsorship letters from our church to the children in Kenya would flow three times a year as our teams went to serve. Upon each team's return, we would have a stack of letters to sift through and send out to the sponsors here at home. The leader of the ministry in Kenya had become almost as well known throughout our church as our own lead pastor. Externally, everything looked great. Internally, there had been concerns. However, the overarching feeling was that the ministry was still working "well enough," and there were no plans to change the model.

It was in 2017 that we began to be confronted with a new reality and new research that would shift our views of how the local church in America could and should care for the vulnerable around the world.

Where we once thought child reunification was never an option for these children, we began to learn that it was not only possible—it was being accomplished in Kenya. Where we were once okay with families sending their children to our group home, we now began to question their circumstances and our approach to serving their community.

We spent time on our knees seeking the Lord about how to proceed, since this ministry was so ingrained into the culture of our church. We lamented the mistakes we made in how we cared for these families. We also rejoiced that there was a Sovereign God who had still brought redemption into the lives of children through this ministry.

In our almost simultaneous lamenting and rejoicing, we began to act. We began to have the hard conversations concerning our partnership and to discern if we could shift from a group home to a transitional program for the children. We also began to seek counsel on how to proceed. We asked for the support of Agape Children's Ministry (a nonprofit that had gone through such a process before us) to give us insight into how to work through the complexity of a transition in care models. They proved to be a huge blessing to us.

While we were initially hopeful that we could make a healthy transition, ultimately, after years of trying, we came to the tough reality that transition was not possible and our partnership needed to end.

It was a tough blow to our church and our brothers and sisters in Kenya, but we knew we had followed God's lead in truly seeking out partnerships that are in the best interest of the families there.

This chapter is entitled "How Now Shall We Serve?" It serves as a rallying cry to the local church in America to begin to honestly and objectively evaluate partnerships. In those evaluations, we must be discerning and not necessarily immediately scrap them if they aren't operating according to the best practices we've been discussing in this book.

Rather, we need to assess our current partnerships and make sure they help us learn and grow together while serving the vulnerable around the world. If they do not, then we prayerfully must seek the Lord in how to move forward.

Partnerships can be a tricky endeavor, but when done well, the power of gospel-centered partnerships moving in the same direction for the good of a community can be incredibly impactful, both for our partners there and for our churches at home.

—Evans Baggs
Pastor of Mobilization and Equipping
Port City Community Church

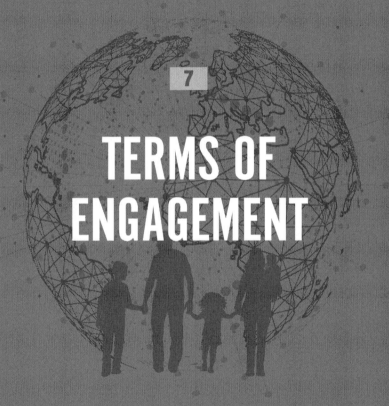

7

TERMS OF ENGAGEMENT

Now that we've explored the principles of best practice and the particulars of partnership, we turn to our final topic of this book: Common ways Western churches engage in global missions.

Many churches engage in global missions through child sponsorship and short-term mission trips. Because they are such prevalent practices, we wanted to explore them in-depth through the lens of best practices. How does our understanding of attachment, child development, and the continuum of care impact these opportunities? Let's talk about it!

Child Sponsorship

One popular way for our churches in the West to engage with global partners is through child sponsorship programs. Often these programs seem like a "win" for everyone involved: the children receive the basic care they need (nutritious food, education, clothing, etc.) and sponsors can connect their giving to the face of an actual child who benefits from it.

However, child sponsorship has the potential for great good—and great harm. Many organizations are becoming concerned about child protection and ethical storytelling within their programs. Sharing a child's name, photo, birthday, and other personal details in an increasingly digital world can put them at risk. Others question whether it's simply a way of using children's stories to tug at the heartstrings of potential donors.

When partnering with an organization that uses child sponsorship as a funding model, it's important to make sure they're operating in the most ethical way possible. The key is to think critically about any form of engagement with our partners. With the best practice lens you've developed throughout this book, you'll be well equipped to walk through this process!

More Than a Band-Aid

In the same way residential care should never be the default care option, child sponsorship should not be the default funding option for a nonprofit. Organizations that do it simply because, "It works!" or, "Donors love it!" should make us wary. Any program that connects vulnerable children to adults outside the organization should be well-thought-out and carefully designed to provide maximum protection.

Child sponsorship is often a program without an end date—or at minimum, a very long shelf life. If we are truly committed to empowering long-term change and eventually not being needed within a community, we need to ask the deeper questions of our partners: How are they planning for the future? Is there a sustainability goal in place? Will the children of those children that are currently in their program need sponsorship as well? How about their grandchildren?

Otherwise, sponsorship may simply be perpetuating the cycle of poverty; it puts a Band-Aid on the wound without recognizing what caused it.

Sponsorship should be more than a Band-Aid on our end, as well. If it's our only form of engagement with vulnerable children, we must take a hard look at our internal motivation. Is it simply a way for us to check that box on our global engagement form? Or is it a true desire to help and invest in the lives of vulnerable children?

While sponsorship isn't necessarily wrong, it shouldn't be our sole avenue for serving vulnerable children. In order to embody the type of partnership we desire, we must go deeper.

True Transformation

We become involved in sponsorship programs because we truly want what's best for vulnerable children—we want to be a part of showing them the gospel in a real, tangible way. If this is our heart, then it's the call of the church to engage in sponsorship programs that don't just address the symptoms but go deep into the roots of poverty to enact true transformation.

If we want to partner with sponsorship programs that achieve this, we can look for programs that emphasize two main goals:

1.   Program integrity
2.   Child, family, and community empowerment

Programs with these goals will likely be run by organizations that are committed to upholding best practices both internally and externally—leading them to provide the best care possible for the children and families they serve. Be encouraged—those types of programs do exist! The point here is not that child sponsorship is inherently wrong; rather, it's to encourage us to look for signs of health, integrity and best-practices within those programs that ultimately serve children, families and communities most effectively and sustainably.

What does this look like in practice? While it can take many forms, here are ten key points to look for in any sponsorship program you decide to support.

Signs of a Healthy Sponsorship Program

1. **Holistic Care:** It considers the physical, emotional, cognitive, and spiritual needs of the children, families, and communities they serve. Children of all abilities, races, religions, and ethnicities are eligible to receive services.

2. **Child Input:** It allows children and their caregivers to have a voice in their participation, and acts on that feedback.

3. **Transitional Plans:** It prepares children for a life of independence after sponsorship and supports families and communities in preparing for a future where sponsorship is no longer necessary.

4. **Family and Community Strengthening:** It is primarily run by national staff who aim to keep families and communities unified (or reintegrated) whenever possible.

5. **Healthy Interaction with Children:** It is informed by current research on adversity and attachment. It works to actively protect and strengthen healthy attachment between children and their caregivers and limit interactions between child sponsors or short-term mission team members. It encourages sponsors to have a positive but realistic view of their role in the children's lives, discouraging feelings of ownership or a "savior complex."

6. **Child Protection:** It implements policies that protect children against abuse and exploitation, and promote a safe environment where children can thrive.

7. **Monitoring and Evaluation:** It regularly tracks and records progress in children's health and development to identify areas for improvement and make any necessary changes to become more effective.

8. **Financial Responsibility:** It offers accurate information on the use of funds and doesn't

allow fundraising considerations to encourage unnecessary placement or prolonged participation of children in the program. It can be helpful to see if they are accredited through organizations like ECFA or Charity Navigator.

9. **Cultural Sensitivity:** It represents different cultures in a positive and honoring way, always striving to learn from and empower local communities. It treats national staff as cultural experts who help navigate the complexities of cross-cultural ministry.

10. **Communication and Storytelling:** It communicates in a way that protects and honors vulnerable children, as well as their families and communities by limiting or altering information (such as names, photos, locations, and ages) revealed about the children in their program and conveying stories with dignity.

A PASTOR'S PERSPECTIVE

[The missionaries we support] practice family-based care. This looks like supporting, educating, and empowering families to keep their children and making sure true orphans (which we also have) remain in their villages. All of these children are supported with sponsorships from our church that include enrollment in our local Christian school, meal support, and access to medical care so that they can stay in a family-based environment. This leads them to secondary school and vocational training so they are not only equipping themselves for a brighter future, but empowering their family as well.

—Aaron

Pastor

A sponsorship program that follows these principles is actively pursuing the ongoing process of becoming a healthy, sustainable model that "meets the needs of the present without compromising the ability of future generations to meet their own needs."[33] Your church can partner with them with confidence, knowing that your partnership can help bring about true transformation for the child, their family, and their community.

> *Adapted from CAFO's booklet,* Guidelines for Healthy Sponsorship Programs, *online at* missionwisebook.com. *The booklet includes an audit to help you assess a sponsorship program, additional case studies, resources, and more.*

Short-Term Missions

Short-term mission trips are another common way we engage with our global partners. Prior to the COVID-19 pandemic, around one million Christians were participating in a short-term mission (STM) trip every year.[34] Although these trips are a relatively recent phenomenon, they've become one of the most popular methods for the Western church to engage globally and connect with what God is doing around the world.

However, like sponsorship, short-term mission and vision trips carry with them the potential for both great good and tremendous harm, especially when we interact with children who lack the protection and connectedness of family.[35]

If you've led or participated in one of these trips, you may have felt uncomfortable at some point during the trip. Not the typical discomfort of being far from home in a new culture, but the discomfort that prompts you to ask, "Am I actually making a difference here?"

Nearly everyone who takes a short-term mission trip has good intentions and longs to improve the lives of others, especially orphans and vulnerable children. However, without wisdom, caution, and a solid understanding of best practices, we can easily cause more harm than good.

It's important to have the right structures in place so that your short-term trips can produce long-lasting good. Once again, good intentions are simply not enough! Scripture says we must consider with wisdom and knowledge what it will take to build something sustainable before we actually start building it. Otherwise it's in danger of not lasting very long.[36] It is only through thoughtful consideration, learning, planning, and implementing that the benefits of short-term missions can overcome the potential pitfalls and obstacles. That's what this chapter is all about.

> *If you want to learn more about the importance of preparation in short-term missions, check out the CAFO infographic,* Short-Term Service Trips, *online at* missionwisebook.com.

Setting the Stage: Seeing Children in Context

Whenever we seek to serve children, we always need to see them in context. Even when they aren't currently part of a family, they are always a part of a larger community.

In an ideal world, God's heart and design is that a child would be surrounded by multiple layers of protection and provision, all interwoven and working together. If one of those layers is removed, either temporarily or permanently, another one could absorb the gap. But imagine if two . . . three . . . four of those layers are removed . . . Take a look at the circles in the infographic on the following page to see how big the gap quickly becomes.

Soon, the child is on the streets. Government intervention, if it's available, is the only layer of protection left. And while the government often does its best, as we've seen in previous chapters, nothing (not even the church) can replace the love and nurture of a permanent family. God's heart is for children to grow within a family, and every layer of protection is vital in preserving and protecting His design.

God's Heart for Children

Responsibilities of each circle of protection to fulfill God's heart for the child

Loom International

Family

The immediate family is intended to provide protection (emotional, physical, mental, and spiritual,) safety, education, identity, unconditional love, belonging, honor, dignity, and an affirming sense of self for

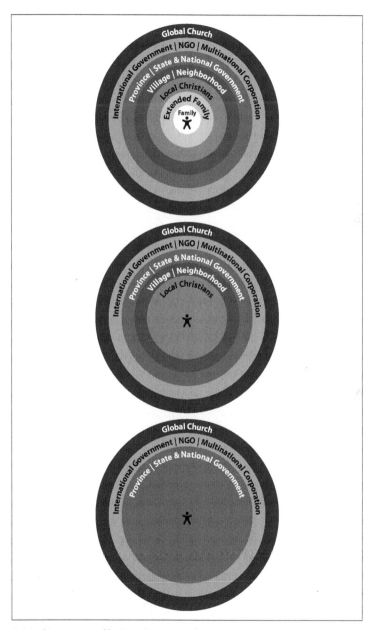

Original images created by Loom International

the child. God's love/grace/discipline is modeled; independence is nurtured and practiced; relationships are modeled with God and people; work skills, conflict resolution skills, etc. are gained.

Extended Family
The extended family is intended to provide the awareness that the child belongs to a bigger world, greater experience in relationship and commitment, support and encouragement for the immediate family, a safety net in case of loss or abuse, and a continued sense of belonging and identity.

Local Christians
Local Christians affirm dignity and honor; provide biblical principles for nurturing a child; and offer love, encouragement, and acceptance of the child/ family. They model the gospel; train in the ways of God; show God's principles integrated in life; support and encourage the family; influence on behalf God's principles in government, business, education, media, etc. for the purpose promoting God's intentions for the family/child; and provide a further sense of belonging, safety, being heard, affirmed, accepted, and participating in the mission of God.

Neighborhood/Community/Village
Intended to provide protection/safety/identity, family support with systems of healthcare, education, social services; just laws that control and protect business/

jobs that support the family; child protection laws; laws against corruption, exploitation, and abuse; laws and systems that encourage, affirm, honor, and give dignity; and an environment of health, beauty, and order.

State/Province/National Government
Intended to provide laws and systems that protect and create options for a world beyond the child's parents; citizenship, participation, setting standards of integrity, economics, wealth creation, land rights, health, social welfare; laws that are just—protecting the rights of all (inheritance, wages, working conditions).

International Governments, NGOs, Multinational Corporations
Protects from and advocates against exploitation when the first layers fail, against exploitation such as debt, unfair economic burden on family; promotes income generation, fair wages, just entrance into the market, dignity for the smallest, weakest, poorest, and neediest. They defend and amplify the local voice, support just practices, protect against corruption, and provide information, training, and other resources.

Global Church
The global church protects, trains, learns, and advocates globally on behalf of the child, working through relationships with local Christians and sharing resources and assets. As a ministry leader,

chances are that you fit in this circle! Take a look at the chart again. What does your relationship to the rest of the circles tell you about what your relationship with the child, family, community, and local church should look like?

The best kind of short-term mission trip integrates these circles of protection by working through the existing layers around a child and supporting efforts to fill in the gaps with local, long-term solutions. Instead of seeking to directly care for the child, it's often most beneficial to build up the support system around them. In this way, we are going "upstream" to solve the problem before a child becomes vulnerable, and we are protecting the safety and attachment of a child who's currently vulnerable.

Going Upstream

"Imagine a large river with a high waterfall. At the bottom of this waterfall hundreds of people are working frantically trying to save those who have fallen into the river and have fallen down the waterfall, many of them drowning. As the people along the shore are trying to rescue as many as possible one individual looks up and sees a seemingly never-ending stream of people falling down the waterfall and begins to run upstream. One of the other rescuers hollers, 'Where are you going? There are so many people that need help here.' To which the man replied, 'I'm going upstream to find out why so many people are falling into the river.'"[37]

Before planning your next trip, it can be helpful to meet with your partners and ask them some questions: How can you best support the work local churches are doing with children and families? How about the community as a whole? The families in the area? Our impact can increase exponentially when we support local Christians working in their neighborhoods and in every area of society to strengthen each circle on behalf of families.

Remember, it's okay to be invisible. By looking at how we can support these circles of influence, rather than organizing an elaborate Vacation Bible School or taking the children to the zoo, we can have a long-lasting impact that deepens our partners' roots in the community and brings generational change.

So what does this look like?

Serving for Empowerment

In order to empower local leadership to lead the trip in the way that's most beneficial for their community, every short-term mission trip should have three goals:

- To listen
- To learn
- To build relationships

However, many teams participate in a trip with one unspoken goal: to accomplish a tangible task—to paint a wall, build a playground, or host an event. If we don't leave the trip with proof of how and where our time was spent, it's easy to feel as if the entire trip was a waste. While this certainly can be an outcome of a clash of cultures, it can also be the result of a clash of priorities.

It's important we recognize that our Western culture tends to prioritize accomplishing tasks while many other cultures place a higher value on relationships than on productivity or outcomes. While both parties may share a desire for effective short-term missions, what does "effective" mean to each one? If we ask that question of our partners, we might be surprised at their answer. Understanding priorities can help both of us walk away from a trip considering it a success.

So how can we realign those priorities and engage in trips wisely to accomplish the empowerment we desire? The following are a few core principles to get us started.

1. **Prioritize child protection.** Safeguarding children from harm should always be our number one priority. It's vital that both we and our partners have robust child protection policies that everyone participating on the trip has read and agreed to abide by during the trip. Background checks should also be conducted on each participant.

2. **Consider your impact on attachment.** Remember
    earlier in this book, when we talked about the importance
    of a consistent caregiver in the life of a child? This is
    especially important for children who've experienced
    trauma. Having team members come and go can harm
    the attachment between a child and their caregiver
    and create a string of broken attachments in the child's
    life. While on your trip, it's important to support the
    bonds between children and their primary caregiver—
    not insert yourself between them. It's wise to avoid
    deep emotional connections with any child. Make sure
    caregivers are meeting the children's primary needs—
    especially in daily routines and intimate moments.
    (This is especially true for infants and children under
    the age of three, as this is a critical time for attachment
    to form!) It can be helpful to set the boundaries and
    expectations clearly ahead of time, so team members
    understand the "why" behind these rules.

3. **Honor parents and primary caregivers.** Caregivers
    will be with the children long after we return home.
    Supporting and honoring them is the best way to
    support and honor children! Before the trip, ask your
    partners how you could best honor them, and then abide
    by their wishes. This means giving gifts or interacting
    with children only with their prior consent and within
    the boundaries they set.

4.   **Uphold families as the ideal.** By now, we can agree: residential care is never the ideal situation for a child. Rather, the ideal place for a child to grow and flourish is in a loving, stable family. By keeping this thought at the forefront of our mind as we plan a short-term missions strategy, we will honor the children who are impacted by our work and those who serve them. In situations where we have a standing relationship with a partner in which we volunteer in a residential center or children's home, this might require small changes to expand our impact. For example, rather than doing a Vacation Bible School or English camp in the home, we can partner with a local church to make it a community-wide offering. This can accomplish multiple purposes:

- We can invite children and caregivers from the home, helping them to develop relationships in the community.
- We can invite vulnerable children and families from the community, supporting their well-being.
- We can empower the local church to be the hero of the story, rather than us.

5.   **Support the community.** Often, the most effective way to meet the needs of children is to invest in the local community capable of protecting and nurturing them over time. This includes their families, schools,

churches, businesses, and local government. You're likely already partnering with one of these entities. If not, consider pouring into these structures instead of an orphanage or children's home—allowing children to be reintegrated into the community instead of separated from it. Always consider what effect it would have on the community if the activities and relational interactions of your trip were repeated by other teams over time. Would it build the kind of community you and your partners have been praying for?

6. **Set clear expectations.** When team members understand, before they even board the plane, that their role is to encourage and empower local leadership, they are better prepared to make the most out of their trip. In fact, in a current study, team members who received the most training and preparation were the most satisfied with their trip experience.[38] Teaching your team members about attachment, child development, and trauma can also help them understand why they won't have personal contact with children during the trip.

7. **Anchor every trip in long-term partnerships.** It's important to root all service in long-term relationships with trustworthy local partners and multiyear ministry plans, and to help trip participants understand why this matters. We can learn from reliable on-the-ground

allies how we can best contribute to their efforts to meet needs in their community over time. The work we've already done in evaluating our current and future partners sets the foundation for this crucial step.

8. **Commit to learning before doing.** Thoughtful education prior to, during, and after a trip is critical to preventing harm. It is also key to making a trip a truly life-transforming experience for participants. We can educate team members on all of the previous principles long before they set foot on the ground where our partners are serving.

Adapted from CAFO's booklet, Wise Short-Term Missions, *online at* missionwisebook.com.

If you want to learn more about wise short-term trips, take a look at the Standards of Excellence in Short-Term Missions' Seven Standards *(online at* soe.org/7-standards*); OVC* Guide *(online at* soe.org/free-downloads/ovc-guide*); and* Faith to Action's *Short-Term Missions Guidance (online at* faithtoaction.org/missions*). You can also explore CAFO's* Global Engagement and the Church *booklet, online at* missionwisebook.com.

Getting Started

So what do these principles look like in real life? How—practically—can we harness the great good that can come from these trips while minimizing risk of harm? As a starting point, we have gathered some alternatives and case studies. This is by no means an exhaustive list! As you consider how these ideas might be applicable for your church and/or mission partners, we hope they can be a catalyst for your own innovations in wise, effective short-term missions.

- **OVC Conference:** Inspire, equip, and connect local citizens with a conference focused on care for orphans and vulnerable children.

  In some cultures, the idea of caring for a nonbiological child as your own may be a foreign concept, even in the church. Even where orphan care is a common concept, local citizens may never have had the opportunity to gather together to learn more about this topic. Work with local partners who are already excited about caring for vulnerable children to host churches, parents, child welfare workers, and other individuals who care for vulnerable children. A conference setting like this has the potential to catalyze long-term change and relationships long past the time the visiting team returns home.

World Orphans—Church Partnership Trip

World Orphans operates with a church partnership model, so all trips occur within the context of a long-term relationship. Teams engage with church partners to learn from and encourage them in their care of orphaned and vulnerable children through community-based family care.

Purpose

To strengthen church partnerships through building relationships and serving together in a mutually beneficial capacity. This trip cares for orphaned and vulnerable children by building up that church and community members caring for them on a regular basis.

Activities

Time with church leadership, learning from leaders of the home-based care program, community meals, home visits (where appropriate), a cultural experience.

Preparation

Prior to the trip, volunteers are provided training via resources like a World Orphan's handbook, Helping Without Hurting in Short-Term Missions *by Steve Corbett and Brian Fikkert,* Slow Kingdom Coming *by Kent Annan, and* Western Christians in Global Mission *by Paul Borthwick.*

These trips are fairly brief (less than one week), as it is better to have a short trip than to be in-country longer than is helpful to a host. Follow up is ongoing, as churches have quarterly video calls with each other and regular trips.

- **Sports:** Incorporate a love for sports to cross language barriers and cultural differences.

  Playing sports is a worldwide pastime and can put volunteers and the members of the communities receiving them on equal footing. A camp offering different types of sports so that children may learn and continue to grow in their skills can be an asset to all involved. Working with the local church will ensure the camp is delivered in a culturally appropriate way, and that ministry can continue long after the short-term team has returned home.

- **Advocacy:** Use a short-term trip to prepare long-term advocates to tell the story of the ministry.

  One of the greatest challenges for most nonprofit ministries is raising awareness of their work and developing partnerships. Inviting key influencers, advocates, and partners to see the long-term work on the ground, as well as giving them insights into the behind-the-scenes operations, can prepare them to be a voice connecting others to the ministry. This trip will also consist of helping them develop a clear vision and strategy for their role as advocates, giving them tools and resources to share, and sharing examples of how to successfully share a story in order to build awareness and catalyze action.

Abide Family Center—Storytelling Trip

Short-term volunteers capture images and stories of Abide families, in order to share the ministry of the organization and celebrate stories of success. In addition to providing material for future fundraising and advocacy, storytellers are trained to be capable of advocating for vulnerable children within their own network upon their return home.

Purpose

Build relationships and train advocates for a locally led family strengthening program, with a goal of encouraging staff and sharing the vision and ministry more broadly.

Activities

Training, relationship building with staff, "staff spoiling day," meet clients at their home to hear their stories and learn about their businesses, work with a client and staff member to refine a narrative. Each home visit will involve a staff member and no more than two team members. The trip ends with an Abide graduation and team debrief, followed by cultural experiences that intentionally support locally-owned businesses.

Preparation

Prior to the trip, each team member signs the Ethical Storytelling Pledge. In the months leading up to the trip, participants communicate through a shared Facebook group where trip leaders post articles and stories to start discussions and reflection, including Urban Halo by Craig Greenfield, The Social Media Guide from Radi-Aid and Barbie Savior, and the Irina Project's tips for interviewing trauma survivors. During the trip, team members receive training using resources from Ethical Storytelling (ethicalstorytelling.com), and discuss these issues with locals and non-locals.

Giving someone permission to tell your story is powerful. Abide strives to avoid misrepresentation, retraumatization, and accidental harm, but also recognizes mistakes happen. Trained mental health professionals supervise all interaction with clients to limit risk of harm. The goal is for all participants to feel that a true and dignified story has been told that empowers and celebrates the family at its center.

The most essential component to trip success is screening team members and the clients thoroughly, including trauma history, readiness to tell their story, and possible consequences to their business. Team members need to be willing to challenge themselves to be better storytellers and open to questioning how they—and others—have done things in the past. Successful participants embrace the saying "when we know better, we do better."

- **Mentors:** Give caring adults the skills to be change makers and disciple makers in the lives of orphaned and vulnerable children.

  In order to grow and develop well, all children need long-term, supportive adult relationships in their lives. However, many children around the world are lacking a sufficient number of safe, caring adults willing to invest in their well-being. Especially for children who may not live in stable, nurturing families, mentors can be a lifeline, offering friendship, guidance, support, and connection. Furthermore, mentors can make a substantive difference in the ability to succeed for children aging out of alternative care, making a healthy mentor relationship a strong protective factor for orphans and vulnerable children in almost any care setting. Working with members of the local church, short-term teams can provide information and resourcing to help train up mentors for the long-term support of vulnerable children.

- **Language:** Use language and culture to facilitate listening, learning, and building relationships.

   In many cultures around the world, learning another language can be a valuable skill. Furthermore, learning about the host country's language and culture can be a worldview-shifting experience for trip participants. This makes a language and cultural exchange a mutually beneficial option. Working through local partners, teams can be one part of a longer-term plan for curriculum, ensuring they master and deliver their part of the curriculum, all within the context of what other teams are teaching.

- **Father and Son:** Host a father and son event that strengthens bonds and cements identities in Christ. For those who don't have a present father, father figures are also welcome.

   In many cultures, the role of a father, although uniquely important, is often quite tenuous. Nonetheless, Scripture and reams of research both indicate that a secure relationship with a father can make all the difference in the life of a child. This event provides an opportunity for visiting father and son teams, as well as father-son pairs from the host community, to grow together in Christ as they explore the biblical model for manhood in Christ.

- **Fundraising:** Utilize a physical challenge in another part of the world to raise awareness and funding for long-term ministry.

    Around the world, incredible ministries are limited from becoming all that they could be by a lack of funds. A short-term team participating in a triathlon, 5K, or mountain climb can be an unprecedented opportunity to highlight needs and opportunities, share the story of the ministry, and raise funds that will empower them to do the best for vulnerable children and families for years to come.

- **Camp:** Help foster and adoptive families build memories together.

    At times, it can seem isolating to be a foster or adoptive family. Others may not understand the behavior of children from hard places or the need to structure life in an unusual way. Planning and hosting a camp for foster and adoptive families can create opportunities to bond and have fun, all with other families who understand. It can also help local churches identify families that might need extra support and how best to minister to them.

- **Skills:** Provide support and skills training to community members, building up the people and systems that care for vulnerable children on a long-term basis.

    All around the world, Christians care for vulnerable children as a result of God's love for us. However, caring for children who have experienced trauma, adversity, and separation from parents can be far more complicated than we anticipate and can require tools and knowledge that may not be readily available in a given context. Short-term teams can support long-term partners providing training on felt needs like trauma-informed care, parenting, family strengthening, or any number of topics that can serve orphans and vulnerable children by building capacity in the families and communities that are involved in long-term care.

Back2Back Ministries—Parent Support Trip

Short-term visitors support long-term family strengthening efforts by channeling ministry efforts into existing programs.

Purpose

To involve the body of Christ in encouraging and building up communities, as a means of strengthening families and keeping them together. In the process, missions teams are educated on the complexity of poverty and trauma and how the gospel moves followers of Christ into that story as agents of change.

Activities
Participating in English or skills classes with local moms, putting on a celebration for local families, visiting families to pray for them (especially those without support), participating as consumers in a "Mom's Market," where moms from the Strong Families program can test handmade products that they could eventually sell elsewhere.

Preparation
Prior to the trip, volunteers are asked to prepare activities for their trip, from a skills class to a devotional to a creative workshop to give at the community center. Optionally, teams can watch Poverty Cure (povertycure.org), or read When Helping Hurts by Steve Corbett and Brian Fikkert or Slow Kingdom Coming by Kent Annan to prepare. During the trip, participants are trained on the nature and impact of poverty, as well as trauma competent care, as all families served have some history of trauma.

Strong, long-term relationships between ministry staff and local families are vital for this type of trip *to be effective, allowing interaction without creating dependency or a culture of poverty tourism. Also critical is education around the importance of communicating dignity to local families. All people experience poverty in one way or another, and there is no "us" and "them."*

- **Social Workers:** Bless and encourage the unsung heroes in caring for vulnerable children—social workers.

    Social work is an exhausting, demanding, and often thankless job. Skilled professional social workers are also critical to the well-being of vulnerable children. Encourage and empower the local church to develop relationships with and support local social workers. Activities could vary widely, but could include anything from a breakfast, honoring local, child-welfare workers; to written thank-you notes and prayers, to tangible gifts to use during their late nights and long days of travel.

- **Pastors Conference:** Empower local pastors through biblical training opportunities and resources on church leadership.

    Often pastors in low-resource countries do not have access to the many tools that are at our fingertips. A quick Google search allows us to explore Greek and Hebrew translations, thousands of commentaries, and multiple versions of the Bible for comparison. Short-term teams (who are themselves equipped on these topics) can help equip local pastors for long-term ministry by offering training on topics like caring for vulnerable children and families, counseling, theology, preaching, building healthy marriages, parenting, and more.

Buckner International—Family Strengthening/Marriage Retreat

Strengthening families identified as in need of extra support by program staff, and offering an opportunity for coaching and capacity building.

Purpose

To connect the church to opportunities to share faith, provide hope, and demonstrate love to vulnerable children and families. Short-term teams support the long-term ministry goals related to family strengthening that occurs through Family Hope Centers by offering a seminar under the guidance and leadership of program social workers and family coaches.

Activities

Prior to the trip, program staff determines and requests activities to address certain concerns or issues within the families who will attend the event. The team will then hold a half-day or one-day seminar/retreat for couples and families. If the missions team has a counselor, they will lead the retreat. Otherwise, lay leaders from the team will lead, under the guidance of program social workers.

Preparation

Every team that serves with Buckner is assigned a missions coordinator that plans the details of the trip with the team contact and in-country staff. Each team has at least one orientation (either in-person or by phone) that includes an overview of Buckner, details of logistics, ministry details, as well as providing each team with a copy of Helping Without Hurting in Short-Term Missions *by Steve Corbett and Brian Fikkert that the team can use to prepare for their trip. A Buckner employee, trained to manage and lead teams, accompanies each team to oversee logistics, communications with in-country staff, manage finances, and serve team members throughout the team's ministry time.*

These are just a few examples of how short-term missions can be creatively repurposed to accomplish the greatest good for our partners and the children they serve. Use them as springboards for your own brainstorming—and don't forget to include your partners in the process! Their insight can lead the conversation in directions we may never have considered.

Putting these principles into practice will lay a solid foundation for a short-term mission experience that benefits everyone involved.

> *If you want to learn more about creative alternatives for short-term mission trips, including more case studies, take a look at CAFO's booklet,* Alternative Models for Short-Term Missions, *available online at* missionwisebook.com.

A Word about Media

As we participate in short-term missions, part of the experience is sharing our trip with others. It's important to share any media (social or otherwise) with the utmost care, especially when they are the stories or images of vulnerable children.

While it may seem harmless to share candid words or photos from your trip in public places, the reality is much more complicated for vulnerable children. In our digital world, it's easier than ever to upload a photo of a child on your social media page and watch the "likes" accumulate. However, it's important to consider the potential harm these posts can cause.

Many vulnerable children have experienced abuse, and some have even been trafficked. There can even be ongoing legal cases involved. All of them have been at-risk in one way or another. Sharing their name, face, location, or other information could put them even more at risk. (Even if you don't explicitly state your location, many phones and social media sites geotag your photos unless you turn this feature off.)

Good Intentions, Real Danger

Especially in today's world, privacy can be quickly lost. Sharing an image on social media means it is in the archives of the internet forever, even if it is deleted. Sharing a story in an email newsletter means that everyone who reads it shares a tiny piece of it, and it no longer belongs to the child or family at the center of the story. Sharing information can even quickly become dangerous. Imagine the following:

A missionary raises support using Facebook and Instagram. Of course, she shares where she will be and what she will be doing:

- *Living in [Name of city, Name of country]*
- *Working at [Name of orphanage or children's home]*

> *She raises support, moves, and begins ministry. In order to share stories of what she is doing with supporters, she posts occasional pictures of children in the home, some with her, some by themselves. She may or may not use names. She is a good person, and just wants to share the story of what God is doing to care for the vulnerable.*
>
> *But now, we have a picture of a child who lives in a certain children's home, in a certain city, in a certain country. And no matter how secure she thinks her account is, it is not—we live in an age when any page can be hacked at any time. Countless people could find access to this information. Without meaning to, she has placed this child at risk.*

While this isn't intended as a scare tactic, it is good to be aware of these dynamics at play. While we may not intend to harm a child, we also may not fully consider the far-reaching consequences of what we share online. It's important to think through these implications and put guidelines in place before we are faced with a decision in the moment!

Photos, videos, and stories of any person or child should be created and shared only in ways that respect their wishes and affirm their dignity as beings made in the image of God. Always gain the consent of the individual, child, or parent before sharing and make sure to limit or alter the information you share.

Also, it can be helpful to consider how the presence of a camera alters our interactions with those we meet. Thinking through the motivation behind each shot will help us stay present and focused on those who are in front of us. It might be helpful to appoint one team member as the photographer each day, freeing up the rest of the group to simply engage in the work you're doing.

And finally, one helpful way to consider the use of our photos, stories, and other media is to ask ourselves a similar question to the one we posed in the chapter about residential care: "If this were my child, how would I want this situation to be handled?" Many of us are very protective of what we share online about our families and our children, and who has access to that information. Considering how we would feel about a stranger posting information about our own child online can help us make a decision that honors the children and families we meet, both during our trip and beyond.

If your partner organization doesn't already have a formal media policy, it's important to develop one together and enforce it with your team members. Not only does this protect vulnerable children and provide dignity to those we serve, it also guards our hearts against the all-too-human temptation to use the experience for our own social gain.

If you want to learn more about media and missions, take a look at CAFO's booklet, Wise and Honoring Representations of Children in Media, *or CAFO's free online course,* Confidentiality, *both available online at* missionwisebook.com.

Who's the Hero? Not Afraid to Be Invisible

A church that can do the most good is one that's willing to be invisible. As we take steps to evaluate and improve our partnerships, and as we seek to serve in light of best practices, we often arrive at solutions that don't center around us.

When we recognize that partnership isn't about getting our emotional needs met (perhaps through admiration of the leadership or recognition on social media or elsewhere), it frees us up to experience our deepest identity in Christ. We then serve and partner out of that deep well, instead of the shallow puddle of self-sufficiency and strategy.

These are not "our" children—they are God's. Beyond that, they belong to their families and communities. Placing God as the hero of the story, and empowering our partners to be the guides for their own communities, will open up incredible opportunities for them to see, hear, and share the gospel in powerful ways.

A Marriage of Equals:
Matching Local and Global Missions

Up to this point, we've been primarily focused on global missions. However, it's important to recognize that the principles of child development, attachment, trauma, and partnership hold true across cultures.

While the cultural nuances may look a little different, the foundational ideas are the same. Best practices for engaging with orphaned and vulnerable children "over there" largely apply to vulnerable children and families "right here"— wherever "here" might be for you. As you partner with local organizations or families in your church serving children in foster care, homeless youth, or other vulnerable populations, keeping these principles in mind can be immensely helpful. And the reverse is also true! It's important to pursue globally what we prioritize locally.

Together, your local and global partnerships should transform and invigorate the life of your church. If we allow it to, our global outreach can change the way we pray, budget, and love our literal neighbors. A short-term mission trip can transform a team member's lifestyle, priorities, ministry engagement, giving . . . even their career choice!

Caring for vulnerable children around the world can also open our eyes to the needs in our own backyard. Often we are eager to help a widow with orphans in Zimbabwe— but what about a single mother down the street? As our heart is broken for one, it begins to soften toward the other.

Engaging in both local and global missions will transform both our inner life and our external actions—if we let it.

Global Missions When the World Is in Crisis

As we move through this world, we experience different crises on a global scale—from natural disasters to pandemics, famines to floods. As believers, this shouldn't surprise us or discourage us, but it should motivate us to compassionate, informed action.

Often, a church's first response to a crisis in another country (especially when we have partners in that country) is to send a missions team. While team members with specific skill sets certainly can be useful in those situations, a trip is often not the most helpful or effective form of relief. And in circumstances like a global pandemic, where travel is severely restricted, it can be close to impossible.

Coordinating the logistics of hosting a team—from picking up the team at the airport, to supplying food and coordinating the schedule—can be a heavy burden on our partners during a trying time. In the best of times, they are happy to put out the effort and carry that burden for the joy and help that it brings in return. But when they are buried under other challenges during a crisis, they likely don't have the capacity to be the kind of hosts they would like to be.

It's important to recognize and honor the potential costs our teams might bring to our partners, especially in a time of crisis. This is not to say that teams are *never* helpful during these moments—only that they are often not the *most* helpful. Be willing to wait, rather than jumping straight into flight reservations the moment borders are open.

This is also another important time to practice open and honest communication with our partners. Have we expressed our willingness to listen? Have we asked them what would be most helpful at this moment? Does our partner feel true freedom to say no to us or to express their genuine needs? If they do request a team, what specific skills do they need?

The answers to these questions might mean we stay invisible and provide financial support, food, or other tangible items. It might mean we recruit all the plumbers in our church to help replumb their facilities. Whatever actions we take, we will be able to listen and respond in a way that empowers and supports our partners during this critical time.

Crises can be a testing point for our partnerships, but they can also be a beautiful opportunity. If we've done the work beforehand to build strong relationships and foster mutual respect and trust, crises can be a unique time to move even deeper into those partnerships as we navigate the challenges together. Knowing they can turn to us and express their true needs will give our partners a solid foundation to recover and rebuild.

As always, our priorities in this should be seeking God's glory, as well as the best interest of the children and families we and our partners serve. Keeping these goals front and center will help us adapt our strategies to respond with flexibility and humility when the world is in crisis.

If you want to learn more about specific opportunities for churches to support organizations impacted by COVID-19, take a look at this CAFO infographic, COVID-19 & Faith Communities, *online at* missionwisebook.com.

If you want to learn more about how COVID-19 is impacting vulnerable children and families around the world, take a look at these recent research infographics published by the CAFO Research Center:

- COVID-19 and Children at Risk
- The Implications of COVID-19 for the Care of Children Living in Residential Institutions
- Rapid Return of Children in Residential Care to Family as a Result of COVID-19

All of these and more are available at missionwisebook.com.

A New Perspective

Perhaps after reading the last few sections, you're beginning to reevaluate the way your church has practiced short-term mission trips or child sponsorship. You may even feel a bit uncomfortable looking back on how things have been done before. Those feelings are completely normal! We are all learning and growing together, and when we know better, we can do better.

However, as we explored in previous chapters, such feelings don't mean we need to completely abandon either form of engagement. There are ways to engage well, to bless our global partners with our presence and support in a way that encourages and empowers them. It just might take a little creativity.

Consider supporting an organization that sponsors families, rather than individual children. Or select an organization that limits the amount of information they share about the children in their program. If you're already engaged in a sponsorship program and this book has brought up concerns, use the chapter about partnerships to guide your conversations with that partner.

In your short-term mission program, explore some of the ideas included in this book or brainstorm one of your own. It might be as simple as moving a VBS program off the site of the residential care center and including both the children and caregivers from the center, as well as working through the local church(es) to include as many children and caregivers in the community as possible. Whatever we can do to support and empower the bond between caregiver and child is a win for them and for us. Likewise, whatever we can do to platform the local church and bring sustainable support to the community long after we're gone is a win for them and for us.

As we begin to think outside the box (something missions pastors and program leaders have had to hone as an essential skill!), we can look forward with excitement to impactful engagement with our global partners— engagement that leads to positive transformation for our church, it's people, and those we serve.

WRAPPING UP AND MOVING FORWARD

Remember, there is so much grace here! As we know better, we can do better. If you're questioning the way you or your church has engaged in global missions in the past, remind yourself that you were doing the best you could within your circumstances. You didn't mess up; you showed up! And showing up is worth celebrating.

As we wrap up this chapter, consider:

- What's one way you or your church have "shown up" for children and families on the topics covered in this chapter? Take a moment to celebrate it!
- What's one thing you learned in this chapter that you feel compelled to share with the rest of your team?
- What's one practical next step you can take to make a small change based on your new knowledge or understanding? (This can be as simple as setting up a meeting with a stakeholder or reviewing one of the resources referenced in this book. Don't overcomplicate things or overburden yourself!)

8

WHAT DO I DO NOW?

In an effort to honor your time and attention, we've packed quite a bit of information into this small book. It will take time to process through it all, explore the additional resources that piqued your interest, and work through the different assessments. We know it's quite a bit, however, it's worth it to take the time to do it well!

You might notice that this section isn't called, "What Do I Do *Next*?" That's because there isn't necessarily one right "next" step for each of you holding this book in your hands. Once you've taken the time to assess where you are with your partnerships, and where you want to go, you can begin with where you are *now* and move forward.

Perhaps your next step is sharing this book with your leadership team or fellow missions pastors, and discussing it together. Perhaps you already have a solid understanding of where your current partnerships stand, and you're ready to begin having conversations with them about the future of your partnerships.

Wherever you are, we encourage you to approach every step with enormous amounts of prayer. John 15 reminds us that apart from Christ, we can do nothing. Our reliance on Him is crucial at every moment and in every circumstance. This is true even—or especially!—in your global missions strategy.

This question is also not one you can answer once, close the book, and be done contemplating. By regularly asking ourselves, "What do I do *now*?" we move along a pathway of continuous growth. Serving children with excellence and incorporating best practices in our ministries will never be a task that is completed. We will never arrive! Instead, it's a lifelong commitment to learning.

Why is it worth it? Because these children are worth it. The gospel is worth it! And seeing the gospel at work in the lives of vulnerable children and their families through the passionate, well-informed service of your church is what we all long to see.

THE EXTRAS

GOING DEEPER

Transitioning to Family-Based Care
Walking Alongside Organizations as They Transition Models of Caring for Children

Throughout this book, we explored the importance of family in the life of a child. We learned that being cared for outside of a family can be harmful for a child's development. Yet the opposite is also true: being cared for within a family, even after prior experience in a residential setting, can be incredibly healing for a child!

It's relatively easy to prioritize family-based care when forming new partnerships. But what if your church is currently supporting an orphanage or a children's home? Now that you know the importance of family, how can you advocate for a change on behalf of the children and organizations you love?

There are many reasons an organization might be running a residential care program. Perhaps they're unaware of the impact it has on a child's development. Perhaps they do understand but feel stuck in their current model, lacking the support and funding necessary to make such a big change.

Whatever the reason, the motivation to change must come from the organization itself—not the pressure you or anyone else places on them.

The process of transitioning from a residential care model to a family-based care model is often referred to as *the transition to family-based care*. As a church and as a partner, you're in a unique position to help organizations in this process. However, it's important to approach it with humility and grace.

The Church's Role

As always, the church's role should start and end with prayer. This is the most important work! Prayer can be followed up with engaging, honest conversations with your partners about their understanding of and convictions toward family-based care. There are several tools at the end of this section that can help you have those conversations.

If your partner decides to begin the care transition process, you can play an important role in that as well. As a church, you are well-positioned to be an advocate, a connector, and supporter in the process. They will need you to be in their corner as a source of encouragement and as a champion for their vision as they begin such a huge task!

As an advocate, you can share with your congregation, and with others, about your excitement for the care transition process. Fostering a positive perspective on these changes can help keep your church engaged, even when that engagement looks different than what they're used to.

As a connector, you can use your access and resources to provide scaffolding for your partners in the process. Residential programs are often well-positioned to transform into family-based care programs. Could the facilities become a community center with after-school programs, business and parenting classes, or other resources aimed at helping keep families together? Do you know individuals who can provide training? Donors who can provide funding? Contractors who can help transform their buildings? Ask your partners what would be most helpful for them.

As a supporter, you can make sure that lack of funding and prayer are not a barrier in the process. Although the operating costs for family-based care are significantly lower than the cost of residential care per child, the initial costs of making the transition can be high.[39] Hiring social workers, retraining current staff, and transforming the purposes of physical buildings takes time and money. Standing behind your partner in a tangible way will communicate the worth and value you see in them and the children they serve.

What Matters Most

While we encourage you to explore the resources at the end of this section, we want to leave you with a few key components of a successful care-transition process. Talking through these important issues with your partner can help deepen your relationship and build positive momentum as you move forward.

1. **Motivated Leadership:** A few motivated individuals often spark the process of care transitions. As the process progresses, motivated leaders are critical to maintaining momentum, overcoming challenges, and remaining steadfast in the goal of transitioning to family-based care.

2. **Stakeholder Partnerships:** Strong, collaborative relationships need to be established with key individuals who have the potential to positively impact the transition process through their unique perspectives, experiences, authority, and connections.

Examples of partner stakeholders include:

- *Agency administrators*
- *Agency direct service providers*
- *Board members*
- *Community leaders*
- *Donors*
- *Local churches*
- *Local community members*
- *Local government officials*
- *National government officials*
- *Transnational intergovernmental leaders*
- *Volunteers*

3. **Culturally-Appropriate Messaging:** It's important to communicate information about care transitions in a way that is consistent with, and respectful of, community norms, values, and expectations. To do this, we must take the time to listen and understand the culture we are engaging with. Our partners will be the experts on this topic!

4. **Intentional Planning:** Purposeful, logical steps toward accomplishing your goal need to be established. This includes an individualized timeline and the flexibility to adapt along the way.

5. **Organizational Restructuring:** Changes to the organizational budget, fundraising, staffing, and programming may all need to be made. This is one area in which you can likely provide the most hands-on support. They will likely lose some donors and supporters in the process. Sticking with them faithfully and helping them educate others on the importance of family-based care can be an enormous blessing.

These five points barely scratch the surface of what's involved in transitioning a program from residential care to family-based care. If this is a topic that has touched your heart and caught your interest, or if one of your partners is interested in beginning to transition their model of care, we encourage you to dive deeper into the resources below.

However, we close this section with a reminder of and a call to do what truly matters most: seeking the heart of God. Prayer is truly key! In care reform, as in all things, our reliance on Him and our desire to do His will should trump all else. Only then will we be able to be effective in the good work we long to do.

Adapted from the CAFO document, What Matters Most in the Transition to Family-Based Care, *available at* missionwisebook.com.

If you want to learn more about helping an organization in the care-reform process, check out these resources:

- *CAFO's booklet* Moving Towards Family Solutions *(online at* missionwisebook.com*)*
- *CAFO's booklet* Transitioning Donors Checklist *(online at* missionwisebook.com*)*
- *Faith to Action's tool* Transitioning to Family Care for Children *(online at* faithtoaction.org/transitioning-to-care-for-children*)*

TOOLS AND STRATEGIES FOR RESTORATION

From Loom International

We encourage you to meditate on the following Scriptures and to create two lists:

1.   One noting what God promises to do
2.   One noting what He asks us to do

Then consider where those responsibilities overlap:

- Where is God calling us to do something that He's also promised to do, creating partnership between us?
- Where is God calling us to do things that He will not do?
- Where is He promising to do things we cannot do?

You can even get creative and draw a Venn diagram!

Scriptures

Isaiah 1:17—**Learn** to do right! **Seek justice, encourage** the oppressed. **Defend the cause** of the fatherless, **plead the case** of the widow.

Deuteronomy 10:18—He **defends the cause** of the fatherless and the widow, and **loves** the immigrant, **giving** him food and clothing.

Deuteronomy 15:11—There will always be poor people in the land. Therefore I command you to **be openhanded** toward your brothers and toward your poor and needy in your land.

Deuteronomy 16:14—**Be joyful at your feast**—you, your sons and daughters, your menservants and maidservants, and the Levites, the aliens, the fatherless and the widows who live in your towns.

Deuteronomy 24:19—When you are harvesting in your field and you overlook a sheaf, do not go back to get it. **Leave it** for the alien, the fatherless and the widow, so that the Lord your God may bless you in all the work of your hands.

Deuteronomy 26:12—When you have finished setting aside a tenth of all your produce in the third year, the year of the **tithe, you shall give it** to the Levite, the alien, the fatherless and the widow so that they may eat in your towns and be **satisfied**.

Psalm 9:8–9—He will **judge** the world in **righteousness**; he will **govern** the peoples **with justice**. The Lord is a **refuge** for the oppressed, a **stronghold** in times of trouble.

Psalm 10:17—You **hear**, O Lord, the desire of the afflicted; you **encourage** them, and you **listen** to their cry.

Psalm 12:5—"Because of the oppression of the weak and the groaning of the needy, I will now arise," says the Lord. "I will **protect** them from those who malign them."

Psalm 35:10—My whole being will exclaim, "Who is like you, O Lord? You **rescue** the poor from those too strong for them, the poor and needy from those who rob them."

Psalm 72:4—He will **defend** the afflicted among the people and save the children of the needy, he will **crush the oppressor**.

Psalm 72:12–14—For he will **deliver** the needy who cry out, the afflicted who have no one to help. He will take **pity** on the weak and the needy and **save** the needy from death. He will **rescue** them from oppression and violence, for **precious is their blood in his sight**.

Psalm 82:3–4—**Defend the cause of** the weak and fatherless; **maintain the rights** of the poor and oppressed. **Rescue** the weak and needy; **deliver** them from the hand of the wicked.

Psalm 107:41—But he **lifted the needy** out of their affliction and **increased** their families like flocks.

Psalm 109:31—For he **stands at the right hand** of the needy one, to save his life from those who condemn him.

Psalm 140:12—I **know** that the Lord **secures justice** for the poor and **upholds the cause** of the needy.

Psalm 146:9—The Lord **watches over** the alien and **sustains** the fatherless and the widow, but he **frustrates the ways** of the wicked.

Proverbs 31:8–9—**Speak up** for those who cannot speak for themselves, for the rights of all who are destitute. **Speak up** and **judge fairly**; **defend** the rights of the poor and needy.

Isaiah 25:4—You have been a **refuge for the poor**, a refuge for the needy in his distress, **a shelter** from the storm and **a shade** from the heat.

Isaiah 40:29—He **gives strength** to the weary and **increases the power** of the weak.

Isaiah 49:13—Shout for joy, O heavens; rejoice, O earth; burst into song, O mountains! For the Lord **comforts** his people and will have **compassion** on his afflicted one.

Isaiah 58:6-7—Is not this the kind of fasting I have chosen: to **loose** the chains of injustice and **untie** the cords of the yoke, to **set the oppressed free** and **break every yoke**? Is it not to **share** your food with the hungry and to provide the poor wanderer with **shelter** – when you see the naked, to **clothe** him, and **not to turn away** from your own flesh and blood?

Isaiah 58:10—If you **spend yourselves** on behalf of the hungry and **satisfy the needs** of the oppressed, then your light will rise in the darkness, and your night will become like the noonday.

Lamentations 2:19—**Arise, cry out** in the night, as the watches of the night begin; **pour out your heart** like water in the presence of the Lord. **Lift your hands** to him for the lives of your children, who faint from hunger at the head of every street.

Ezekiel 34:4—You have not **strengthened the weak** or **healed the sick** or **bound up the injured**. You have not **brought back the strays** or **searched for the lost**. You have ruled them harshly and brutally.

Daniel 4:27—Therefore, O King, be pleased to accept my advice. "**Renounce your sins by doing what is right** and your wickedness by **being kind** to the oppressed. It may be that your prosperity will continue."

Zephaniah 3:19—At that time I will deal with all who oppressed you; I will **rescue the lame** and gather those who have been scattered. I will **give them praise and honor** in every land where they were put to shame.

Matthew 10:42—And if anyone gives **a cup of cold water** to one of these little ones because he is my disciple, I tell you the truth, he will certainly not lose his reward.

Matthew 18:5—And whoever **welcomes** a little child like this in my name welcomes me.

Matthew 18:10—See to it that you **do not look down on** these little ones. For I tell you that their angels in heaven always see the face of my Father in heaven.

Luke 4:18—The Spirit of the Lord is on me, because he has anointed me to **preach good news** to the poor. He has sent me to **proclaim freedom** for the prisoners and recovery of sight for the blind, to **release the oppressed**, to proclaim the favorable year of the Lord.

Acts 20:35—In everything I did, I showed you that by this kind of **hard work we must help the weak**, remembering the words the Lord Jesus himself said: "It is more blessed to **give** than to receive."

Romans 15:1—We who are strong ought to **bear with the failings of the weak** and not to please ourselves.

Galatians 2:10—All that they asked is that we should continue to **remember the poor**, the very thing I was eager to do.

Psalm 25:16—**Turn to** me and **be gracious** to me, for I am lonely and afflicted.

Proverbs 31:20—She **opens her arms** to the poor and **extends her hands** to the needy.

ADDITIONAL RESOURCES

All resources are available free of charge at *missionwisebook.com*

Title	Source	Format
12 Principles on the Place for High-Quality Residential Care and How We Achieve It	CAFO	Booklet
Alternative Models for Short-Term Missions	CAFO	Booklet
Attachment After Adversity	CAFO	Booklet
Building Resilience Through Relationship	CAFO	Booklet
The Changing Brain: Created to Heal	CAFO	Booklet
Child Development	CAFO	E-Course
Child Protection	CAFO	E-Course
Children, Orphanages, and Families	Faith to Action	Booklet
Community Mapping & Partnership	CAFO	Booklet

Title	Source	Format
Confidentiality	CAFO	E-Course
A Continuum of Care for Orphans and Vulnerable Children	Faith to Action	Booklet
The Core Elements: Companion Primer	CAFO	Booklet
Core Elements of Success in OVC Care	CAFO	Booklet
COVID-19 and Children at Risk	CAFO	Infographic
COVID-19 & Faith Communities	CAFO	Infographic
Engaging Local Cultures	CAFO	Booklet
Ethical Short-Term Missions & Volunteering	ACCI	Website
Fostering Trust in Collaboration Agreement	CAFO	Document
Global Engagement and the Church	CAFO	Booklet
Guidelines for Healthy Sponsorship Programs	CAFO	Booklet
How Childhood Trauma Affects Health Across a Lifetime	Ted Talk	Video
Implications of COVID-19 for the Care of Children Living in Residential Institutions	CAFO	Infographic
Moving Towards Family Solutions	CAFO	Booklet
On Understanding Orphan Statistics	CAFO	Booklet

Title	Source	Format
OVC Guide	SOE	Booklet
Partnership Agreement Template	CAFO	Document
Partnership Review Template	The Partnering Initiative	Document
Rapid Return of Children in Residential Care to Family as a Result of COVID-19	CAFO	Infographic
Seven Standards of Excellence	SOE	Article
Short-Term Missions Guidance	Faith to Action	Booklet
Short-Term Service Trips	CAFO	Booklet
Transitioning Donors Checklist	CAFO	Booklet
Transitioning to Family Care for Children	Faith to Action	Booklet
What Matters Most in the Transition to Family-Based Care	CAFO	Document
When Helping Hurts	Steve Corbett and Brian Fikkert	Book
Wise and Honoring Representations of Children in Media	CAFO	Booklet
Wise Short-Term Missions	CAFO	Booklet
Wise Short-Term Missions (Course)	CAFO	E-Course

ENDNOTES

1. Antecedents to Child Placement in Residential Care: A Systematic Review, https://docs.google.com/document/d/11Ym373OlwyLs GKD9CFFtWYv2GHn9OaXGAacSzmXIcoo/edit.

2. C. Wildeman, F. R. Edwards, and S. Wakefield, "The Cumulative Prevalence of Termination of Parental Rights for U.S. Children, 2000–2016," *Child Maltreatment*, 25, no. 1, 32–42, https://doi.org/10.1177/1077559519848499.

3. F. S. Martin and G. Zulaika, "Who Cares for Children? A Descriptive Study of Care-Related Data Available through Global Household Surveys and How These Could Be Better Mined to Inform Policies and Services to Strengthen Family Care," *Global Social Welfare*, 3 (2016), 51–74. https://doi.org/10.1007/s40609-016-0060-6.

4. UNICEF.

5. Waddoups, Anne Bentley, et al. "Developmental Effects of Parent–Child Separation." *Annual Review of Developmental Psychology*, vol. 1, no. 1, 2019, pp. 387–410., doi:10.1146/annurev-devpsych-121318-085142.

6. "Toxic Stress," Harvard Center on the Developing Child, https://developingchild.harvard.edu/science/key-concepts/toxic-stress.

7. "Excessive Stress Disrupts the Architecture of the Developing Brain: Working Paper No. 3," National Scientific Council on the Developing Child, last modified 2014, http://developingchild. harvard.edu/resources/reports_and_working_papers/.

8. 1 Corinthians 12.

9. Romans 12:2.

10. V. J. Felitti et al., "Relationship of Childhood Abuse and Household Dysfunction to Many of the Leading Causes of Death in Adults," *American Journal of Preventive Medicine*, 14, no. 4 (1998), 245–58, https://www.ajpmonline.org/article/S0749-3797(98)00017-8/fulltext.

11. Harvard Center on the Developing Child. (2017). Stress derails healthy development. Retrieved from https://developing child.harvard.edu/resources/toxic-stress-derails-healthy-developmentarabic-subtitles/

12. Teicher, M. H. & Samson, J. A. (2016). Annual research review: Enduring neurobiological effects of childhood abuse and neglect. Journal of Child Psychology and Psychiatry 7: 241–266. doi:10.1111/jcpp.12507

13. P. Granqvist and L. A. Kirkpatrick, "Religion, Spirituality, and Attachment," in *APA Handbook of Psychology, Religion, and Spirituality (Vol. 1): Context, Theory, and Research*, ed. K. I. Pargament, J. J. Exline, and J. W. Jones (American Psychological Association, 2013), 139–55, https://doi.org/10.1037/14045-007.

14. A. McDonald, R. Beck, S. Allison, L. Norsworthy, "Attachment to God and Parents: Testing the Correspondence vs. Compensation Hypotheses." *Journal of Psychology and Christianity*, 24 (2005), 21–28.

15. M. Dozier and M. Rutter, "Challenges to the Development of Attachment Relationships Faced by Young Children in Foster and Adoptive Care," in *Handbook of Attachment: Theory, Research, and Clinical Applications*, ed. J. Cassidy and P. R. Shaver (New York: The Guilford Press, 2008), 698–717.

16. K. L. Raby and M. Dozier, "Attachment across the Lifespan: Insights from Adoptive Families," in *Current Opinion in Psychology*, 25 (February 2019), 81–85.

17. Nelson, C. A., Zeanah, C. H., Fox, N. A., Marshall, P. J., Smyke, A. T., & Guthrie, D. (2007). Cognitive recovery in socially deprived young children: The Bucharest early intervention project. Science,318(5858), 1937-1940. doi:10.1126/science.1143921

18. Psalm 68:5–6.

19. M. H. van Ijzendoorn et al., "Institutionalisation and Deinstitutionalisation of Children 1: A Systematic and Integrative Review of Evidence Regarding Effects on Development," *The Lancet Psychiatry*, 7, no. 8 (2020): 703–20, https://doi.org/10.1016/ s2215-0366(19)30399-2.

20. Deuteronomy 10:18; Psalms 10:14; 68:5–6.

21. Isaiah 1:17; Matthew 25:40; James 1:27.

22. C. Csáky, "Keeping Children Out of Harmful Institutions: Why We Should be Investing in Family-Based Care," *Save the Children UK*, 2009, https://resourcecentre.savethechildren.net/ library/keeping-children-out-harmful-institutions-why-we-should-be-investing-family-based-care.

23. D. Seneviratne and F. Mariam, "Home Truths: Children's Rights in Institutional Care in Sri Lanka," in *Children's Rights and International Development*, ed. M. Denov, R. Maclure, K. Campbell (New York: Palgrave Macmillan, 2011) 17–39, https:// doi.org/10.1057/9780230119253_2.

24. S. T. Parwon, Orphanage assessment report submitted to Hon. Vivian J. Cherue, 2006.

25. O. Y. Naumova et al., "Effects of Early Social Deprivation on Epigenetic Statuses and Adaptive Behavior of Young Children: A Study Based on a Cohort of Institutionalized Infants and Toddlers," *PLOS ONE*, 14, no. 3 (2019), https://doi.org/10.1371/journal.pone.0214285.

26. van IJzendoorn, "Institutionalisation and Deinstitutionalisation of Children 1", https://doi.org/10.1016/s2215-0366(19)30399-2.

27. M. H. van Ijzendoorn and F. Juffer, "The Emanuel Miller Memorial Lecture 2006: Adoption as Intervention. Meta-Analytic Evidence for Massive Catch-Up and Plasticity in Physical, Socio-Emotional, and Cognitive Development," *Journal of Child Psychology and Psychiatry*, 47, no. 12 (December 2006), 1228–45.

28. https://research.cafo.org/practice/core-elements/training-modules/partnership-community-mapping/.

29. F. S. Martin and G. Zulaika, "Who Cares for Children? A Descriptive Study of Care-Related Data Available through Global Household Surveys and How These Could Be Better Mined to Inform Policies and Services to Strengthen Family Care," *Global Social Welfare*, 3, no. 2 (April 29, 2016), 51–74, https://doi.org/10.1007/s40609-016-0060-6.

30. Innovations in Care for Children Separated from Parents: Transitioning from Residential to Family Models of Service, https://docs.google.com/document/d/1W11yUx9o4bEmKgJ9t n5t_0W9XAddtLZOIianJJZw4mM/edit?ts=6048f97a.

31. 1 Corinthians 9:22.

32. Matthew 25:40 NIV.

33. Sustainable Development, International Institute for Sustainable Development, https://www.iisd.org/about-iisd/sustainable-development.

34. R. Wuthnow, R., *Boundless Faith: The Global Outreach of American Churches* (Berkley: University of California Press, 2010).

35. C. H. Zeanah et al., "Misguided Altruism: The Risks of Orphanage Volunteering," *The Lancet*, 3, no. 9 (June 26, 2019), https://www.thelancet.com/journals/lanchi/article/PIIS2352-4642(19)30213-5/fulltext.

36. Luke 14:28–30.

37. https://www.upstreamprevention.org/

38. https://issuu.com/christianalliancefororphans/docs/stm_infographic?fr=sYzQ0ZjI1MjI3MjI.

39. B. J. Carroll and N. G. Wilke, "Transitioning Donors: 5 Steps to Bring Your Supporters on the Journey to a New Model," 2019. See https://issuu.com/christianalliancefororphans/docs/5_steps_transition_donors_to_give_t

ABOUT THE AUTHORS

Jason Johnson

Jason Johnson is a former pastor and church planter and has served as the National Director of Church Ministry Initiatives at CAFO since 2015. Jason and his wife, Emily, became foster parents in 2012 and have since become adoptive parents as well. Jason works with churches and organizations around the country on resource development and best practices of engagement in serving vulnerable children, families, and communities. Jason and Emily live in Texas with their four daughters.

Nicole Wilke

Nicole Wilke serves as Director of CAFO's Center on Applied Research for Vulnerable Children and Families. Prior to this role, she worked as a child and family therapist, missionary, in juvenile detention, and with children with special needs. Through her professional and personal life, she has gained extensive experience with foster care, adoption, trauma recovery, and transitioning to family care. Nicole has degrees in psychology, family studies, marriage and family therapy, and permanency and adoption competency. She lives with her family in Peru, where they work to see vulnerable children raised in families.

Laura Nzirimu, Editor

Laura Nzirimu has served in the nonprofit community for almost a decade, managing communications, sponsorship, best practice, and more. She is currently the Digital Marketing Specialist for CAFO's Center on Applied Research for Vulnerable Children and Families. She is passionate about collaborating with others to continually learn more and do better on behalf of children everywhere. Laura and her husband live in the Pacific Northwest.

About the Christian Alliance for Orphans

The Christian Alliance for Orphans (CAFO) unites 200+ respected organizations and a national network of 700+ churches. Our joint initiatives inspire and equip Christians to live out effectively the Bible's call to care for orphans and vulnerable children.

CAFO membership is an opportunity to join in a vision for God's glory and the care of vulnerable children that is larger than any one organization or project. Together, we seek to inspire, interlink, and equip God's people to reflect His heart for the vulnerable. To a watching world, the Alliance is an all-too-rare picture of the church unified, serving the fatherless in both word and deed, bearing poignant testimony to the character of our God.

To learn more, visit *cafo.org.*

About the Research Center

CAFO's Center on Applied Research for Vulnerable Children and Families uses original and curated research and resources to help bridge the gap between theory and practice. The Research Center is a trusted guide for the busy frontline practitioner who wants to provide the best care possible for vulnerable children and families around the world.

**To learn more about the Research Center
and its resources, visit *research.cafo.org.***

About the National Church Ministry Initiative

Through the National Church Ministry Initiative, CAFO helps churches build effective and sustainable ministries with essential knowledge, best-practice models, practical resources, strategic coaching, and networking opportunities.

To learn more about the National Church Ministry Initiative, and how your church can get involved, visit *cafo.org/church.*

Made in the USA
Las Vegas, NV
21 October 2021

32785210R00107